ACC
POWERFUL

"A truly wealthy woman knows how to value the power of the feminine. Rachael Jayne shows you exactly how to increase your personal presence, have deeper relationships, and get back in touch with your sensuality. You deserve to treat yourself to this book."

~Rev. Karen Russo, MBA, award-winning author, *The Money Keys*

"As a fellow professional singer, speaker, and advocate for women's empowerment, I applaud Rachael Jayne's work here, which gives you a comprehensive, heart-centered, step-by-step guide on how to create your authentic feminine presence—the core key, as a woman, to creating what you want in all areas of your life and one that cultivates joy, peace and real power. Brava Rachael Jayne!"

~Lynn Rose, Transformational Speaker, Singer,
TV and Radio Host, Creator of *"The WOW Factor"*

"This book helps a woman marry the two powerful forces of sexuality and spirituality so she can experience more passion in love, and fulfillment in life."

~Caroline Muir, Founder of Divine Feminine –
Awakened Masculine Institute.

"This is an experiential process, not an intellectual one. I have done so much personal and spiritual work, but Rachael Jayne's teachings take it to another level—a very deep and personal level. Rachael Jayne is a testament to the power of this. She has an amazing presence and is a shining example of the results of this work."

~Laurie Silver, Mom, Wife, and a Woman Dedicated to Growth.

"Every woman on the planet will benefit from reading this book; it invokes the true feminine essence of being a powerful woman, simple yet profound."

~Sheree Carbery, Founding Director of *Conscious Women*

"This book opens greater, heart-felt pathways for you to be a living example of feminine essence and deliciously express the qualities that contribute to a passionate and purposeful life. Powerful and Feminine is an invitation to a place of authenticity, where there is nothing to hide. An essential read for women seeking to transcend their perception of personal limitation and discover their vitally important role in world transformation."

~Charlene M. Proctor, Ph.D., author of
Let Your Goddess Grow! and ***The Women's Book of Empowerment***

"The magnetic quality of the 'feminine' can be used to land the perfect job, to have the 'right' person notice you at the 'right' time, or to negotiate calmly with your children. This book gives you the tools and easy practices to do all this and more!"

~Christine Kloser, author of ***The Freedom Formula***

POWERFUL AND FEMININE

How to Increase Your Magnetic Presence and Attract the Attention You Want

RACHAEL JAYNE GROOVER

Published by Deep Pacific Press
117 E 37th St. #580, Loveland, Colorado 80538
(970) 377-2562

2nd Edition, 3rd Printing
March, 2023

ISBN 978-0-9832689-6-3 (paperback)

Library of Congress Control Number: 2019938024

Cover Design by:
Mauna Eichner

Programs by Rachael Jayne Groover

Art of Feminine Presence®

The Awakening®

Awaken Your Impact®

The Awakened Speaker®

Meet Rachael Jayne online and receive free training at:
RachaelJayne.com

DEDICATED

to my mum, Diane Kennedy,
who created a loving and encouraging environment
for all her children and students
to reach their greatest potential,
and to my dad,
Greg Kennedy,
who has been a constant, safe, masculine presence
throughout my life.

Table of Contents

A PREFACE TO THE NEW EDITION

A FEMININE AWAKENING

Someone posted this on my Facebook page recently:

"Rachael Jayne, when you first started shooting videos about feminine power and running classes with the words 'Feminine Presence' in it I thought, 'You're not the type of person to be leading this kind of movement. You didn't have the experience or presence that was needed.' Now I see I was mistaken."

Friends who saw this post immediately private messaged me to make sure I wasn't hurt by this, given it was shared publicly. I wasn't offended. I understood. I wasn't experienced when I started. I wasn't that magnetic. When I first started talking online about women redefining power and the importance of the feminine principle, I frequently thought, "Who am I to be saying I can help women be *Powerful and Feminine?*" I celebrated this social media post by sharing it. Her candid words were proof that what is in this book *works!*

What a difference a decade makes! I've been teaching the material from this book and the *Art of Feminine Presence* trainings for over ten years now. My life looks barely recognizable. The insecurities that directed my life have (almost) all disappeared, and I'm left with an inner peace and a quieting of the mind that I never thought possible. In 2002 I started to practice connecting to my feminine essence after attending my first workshop on the subject. This was right after moving from Australia to America and being immediately dumped on arrival by the guy I thought was "the one." The first impetus to consider this disconnection from my feminine was the trouble I was having attracting the kind of man I wanted as an intimate partner.

Once I woke up to what I truly desired in a partner, embraced my feminine power and in turn met my gorgeous husband, my attention switched to how I could use this work to attract the attention that I wanted from ideal clients, and potential business opportunities. I went from being almost broke, having to move towns after a foreclosure of our home, scared to promote myself and ask for money, to now leading trainings all over the world, speaking to audiences every week, leading a successful company, with two best-selling books, and no anxiety about promoting myself and this work. All the while being happier, healthier, less stressed, and more in love with my husband, family, and friends than I've ever been.

I started reading self-help/spiritual books and meditating in my early twenties. I've been interested in the spiritual awakening process since then. Once I had attracted the man, the career opportunities, and the beautiful new home, my attention switched to being more focused on attracting states of awareness of what some would call "enlightenment." I couldn't say this when the first edition of *Powerful and Feminine* came out, but I can now. The practices in this book and the *Art of Feminine Presence* trainings are a direct path to embodied spiritual realization. By embodied I mean that your spiritual understanding doesn't remain in your head as concepts you know, or that you sense are true. The realization drops down into the body and becomes the experience of overflowing unconditional love, vital energy, freedom of expression, beauty, presence, and non-resistance to whatever is occurring. It's ecstatic joy that radiates through you and into your life.

Not only have I seen radical change in my personal life, but the world has embraced the conversation about the need for the feminine principle to play a more equal part in our evolution. Ten years ago the terms "feminine essence" or "feminine power" were hardly used. The feminine awakening that had to happen was just sprouting. A few people were talking about it, writing about it, and I was one of them (in my own small way). I felt it was an integral topic for transformation because I could see how I, and many other women close to me, had taken on more of a masculine role as we tried to become equal with men. We were embodying more of a masculine essence to stay safe in order to not have to live with an open, undefended heart. After all, we'd been treated as not equal and hurt many times. These days, those same terms are more widely known and used. Every day on my social media feed there is another coach, author, or teacher sharing how being connected to your feminine is important while reaching success in the areas you desire.

I would like to think that this book, which became an international best-seller almost ten years ago, had a little something to do with that. So many people have written to me since then sharing how dog-eared their book has become, marked up with a hundred or more highlights, and that *Powerful and Feminine* was their "women's empowerment bible" of sorts.

In the last ten years women's representation in the United States Congress is higher than it's ever been. There are more women than ever running for President of the United States that display the feminine essence in their campaigns. The Me-Too movement shone light on one of humanity's biggest shadows and changed many working environments forever. Gay marriage rights and more compassion and flexibility about sexual orientation and gender identity are just some of what has occurred that we can celebrate.

Right before the first edition of *Powerful and Feminine* I had just started to teach small weekly classes in my home, which I called *Art of Feminine Presence.* I had devised practices and routines to train my body and my energy awareness which had helped me quickly break through my fear of receiving attention while relaxing into my feminine. This was instrumental in changing my dynamic around dating emotionally unavailable men and led me to marry the man of my dreams. I'd also just started to notice a shift in my ability to speak to groups and attract the attention I wanted in my career with what I was practicing.

I convinced five women I had recently met to be my guinea pigs. I created more experiments and practices and would teach them one per week along with a subtle movement meditation in order to activate the feminine essence in a woman. My goal? For us all to feel unshakeable and magnetic in situations that would have usually put us under stress—like a speech, job interview, or first date. This wasn't about projecting some forced sense of confidence. It was about being so present to the point that self-consciousness completely vanished, and in its place came a fully embodied loving power.

The practices worked immediately—for every one of us. Within six months I had thirty-five women who had come to my living room to learn these practices. (There are forty-four practices in the body of work, many of which need to be done in person and don't translate to a book format.) It was sweeping through the town that we had just moved to because friends of these women were asking, *"What has changed? You are doing something different. You look ten years younger."* They would reply, *"I'm hanging out with Rachael Jayne, learning Art of Feminine Presence."* Within a year of starting weekly classes I was planning my first teacher training in order to get help to share this with more women.

Art of Feminine Presence has now celebrated its 10th year anniversary. I've personally worked with over 12,000 women from different cultures, ages, and spiritual backgrounds, helping them be more visible, courageous, and fully self-expressed. We have over three hundred certified teachers working with us to share this work in companies, prisons, colleges, local yoga studios, and in homes with their friends and other women committed to growing personally.

In this time, I've made some surprising discoveries. Many of these discoveries I've added to this edition because they have profoundly elevated the way I live, love and lead. I've added more detail around how embodying the feminine essence relates to our spiritual awakening. I've shared my answers to some of the toughest debates I've had over the years regarding the word "feminine," and how many think it's an outdated, unspiritual, and detrimental word to use as we attempt to empower women. I've included a chapter on the darker and more toxic side of the feminine that we need to clean up. You'll read and learn from new inspiring stories of women who've taken this work to heart and who've made radical shifts in their lives. I've added a book club and women's group resource page at the end to support you in sharing this with women who you know could benefit.

The subtitle of this book is: *How to Increase your Magnetic Presence and Attract the Attention you Want.* All my life I have wanted attention, but at the same time, I've been frightened of it. I want attention because I know that if

I can't get people's attention and hold it, my relationships suffer, my career suffers, and I suffer. I suffer because attention is like food and water for all human beings. It's essential for happiness and wholeness. I'm frightened of attention because of all the memories of when it wasn't safe to have attention directed towards me.

I'm not alone. I see the desire in so many women's hearts to make a difference—and share their voice and their message. The problem is at the same time they frequently still have the brakes on. If a person doesn't reconcile their fear of truly being seen, and they don't tame the fear of judgment, they'll never be able to fully share their voice. When a voice is shut down, that life gets shut down.

No matter how much you feel shut down in any area of your life, this book is an opening. It's an invitation and a guide for you to become more fully and courageously expressed. My liberation came as I practiced diligently with what we are about to explore here together. We have to reclaim our power, our bodies, and our sexual essence so we aren't so rattled by life. The more rattled we are, the more our rational, resourceful brains take the backseat and our fears take the wheel.

What do women who feel an unshakeable, authentic, grounded presence do? They look for somewhere to give and be of service because their focus is not on staying safe and small or working themselves into the ground or tearing others down. Their focus is on being real, open, and undefended. As a result, they make better leaders, better parents, better teachers, and better lovers.

What would happen if you became a woman who was unshakeable when all eyes were on her? What would you stop putting off?

I'm here to invite you to not put that off any longer.

INTRODUCTION

Light Up the Room

People are like stained-glass windows.
They sparkle and shine when the sun is out,
but when the darkness sets in,
their true beauty is revealed only if there is a light from within.

~Elisabeth Kübler-Ross

Certain women walk into a room and are noticed instantly. These women have an air of confidence and a magnetic quality about them that is attractive to others and seems effortless. Other women are the exact opposite; they often seem invisible and frequently make comments like, "no one remembers I was even there." The difference between these two types of women is that one has "presence" and one does not. The unfortunate reality is most women do not have the level of presence they need to easily gain the attention they want. Most women don't realize what signal they are sending, and many don't have the *authentic* confidence they need to achieve success. My intention, through the information and exercises in this book, is to help you *consistently* be in the first group of women who have a magnetic feminine presence. Whether in the boardroom, the bedroom, the dating room, or the networking room, once you have practiced the exercises in *Powerful and Feminine*, you will be seen and heard in a whole new empowered way. I have seen this shift happen in thousands of women, and it does not matter what age, shape, or size you are; when you finally step fully into your feminine power, your life will change dramatically.

I want you to light up every room you walk into—not because your ego needs a boost, and not because you are in competition for attention and somehow need to win. This book is not about how to manipulate the people around you to be noticed, and it's not about how to project an exaggerated sense of confidence like "old-school" women's empowerment trainings have typically taught. No, I want you to light up the room you walk into because you have something to share with others that is of value. I want you to light up the room you walk into because when a woman walks into a room with a sensually alive body, a compassionate and loving heart, and a peaceful mind, she naturally affects the people around her in the most profound ways; she gives others permission to share their Light. When you are truly powerful *and* feminine, you naturally encourage others to be big, bold, and beautiful in a way that makes them feel comfortable rather than intimidated. The world needs more women like this.

We are seeing a re-emergence of the feminine power right now. It's a movement we all need to get behind. Many women want to step up and make a difference by being an inspiring example of a woman who is powerful *and* feminine. However, when I look around, I see many women whose hearts are aching for love, attention, and appreciation. They feel there is so much inside of them, but don't know how to get it out. This book is written for those women who long to be seen, and who want to open their hearts and be claimed by a strong masculine presence that honors their feminine beauty. This book is for women who are bright, self-sufficient, and committed to their personal growth but who, on the inside, may feel a little hardened and burned out. It's for women who want to experience their tender, succulent, and sensual side but don't know how to reclaim their own deliciousness. It's for women who want to relax into expressing more of who they are. To do this—to embody this internal power and pleasure—we have to learn what it is to be both powerful *and* feminine; to do this, we need to embrace our feminine essence.

A woman's personal power and magnetism grow when she connects with her feminine essence. The day I realized that my feminine essence was one of the most attractive and powerful things about me—not just my intelligence, looks, or optimism—was the day everything shifted for me. I went from being confused about my failed relationships with men, always in competition with other women, and not noticed in the way I wanted, to attracting the love of my life, feeling confident in who I am, and embodying a high level of personal presence that attracts attention—any time I choose to turn it on. It's been quite the journey. I'm excited to share with you all the practices I did to create this shift, as well as my observations and research on those women who embody a magnetic presence and open heart. It's a fun and empowering art that any woman can learn.

Your race, age, religion, political persuasion, and sexual orientation are not of concern to me on this journey; I care only about your honesty and willingness to learn. Throughout this book, I use the word "male" when referring to an intimate partner; this is only for the sake of convenience and is not intended to offend, but to simplify. This book is not primarily intended for men but at the same time does not exclude men either. As most of us are well aware, some men have challenges understanding women; this book can offer significant insight in this regard. It can support a man's own personal growth as well as give him tools to support a woman in his life to be both powerful *and* feminine.

One of the most important pieces of wisdom I ever received was from author and teacher, Caroline Myss: "Do not pick up another book until you have integrated at least five things from the book you just read." Unfortunately, it often happens that we read and enjoy a personal growth book but then don't fully integrate the information into everyday life before we shelve it and open the next one. Several years ago, I made the promise to follow through on what I learned when I read an inspirational book, and as a result I moved from being a motivational self-help book junkie to creating a full and joy-filled life. This is now my invitation to you. Will you make a commitment to integrate at least five things from what you read in this book? Obviously, I'd love you to devour the whole book and make it fully a part of you, but five is a great start.

There are several ways you can use this book. Open it anywhere, and I promise there will be down-to-earth answers waiting for you. Or you can travel through this book from start to finish. In the first section I share what the feminine essence is, why we have disconnected from it, and some of the quickest ways to turn its power and magnetism on. I then describe how the feminine essence can affect your spiritual life and your sexual life, along with practices to deepen your connection to both. I give you my best practices that will increase your radiance and your ability to be seen, followed by the five biggest mistakes women make in relationships with men. I finish with how we can all make a huge difference on this planet if we embody the compassionate, confident feminine energy described in this book. After all, at our core we want to know we matter to others, and we want to serve others. Throughout the entire book, I offer both integration exercises and introspective questions to help you put what you read into practice. If you like, keep a journal of your own thoughts and feelings as you read, or use the *Powerful and Feminine Companion Guidebook* (**www.FeminineGuidebook.com**) to record your progress and deepen your practices. If you feel inspired, ask a woman friend or two to read this book with you so you can discuss the relevance in your own lives.

My grandest hope is that *Powerful and Feminine* will have you question everything you have been taught about what it means to be a powerful woman—that it will help you to make peace with your softness and vulnerability so you can stop living with a guarded heart. My hope is that it will help you to get in your "flow" and not always have to push to make things happen, and that it will accelerate your personal and spiritual development in ways you may never have thought of before.

Are you ready now to light up your life with the vibrancy of your feminine essence? Are you ready to light up every room you walk into? Let's begin our journey, then, by looking first at why the feminine essence is so magnetic and how you can start to use it for your own good, the good of those around you, and ultimately the whole world.

CHAPTER ONE

The Most Attractive Force Within You

Mysteries are feminine; they like to veil themselves but still want to be seen and divined.

~Karl Wilhelm Friedrich Schlegel

The bumper sticker on my first car proclaimed, "*Single and Loving It!*" The last thing I wanted to be known as was a woman whose life revolved around her "man." I was irritated by women who ditched their friends as soon as a man came into their life. After all our mothers and grandmothers had given up for us, hadn't we women come a little further than that? But I was not like those women. While dating in my late teens and early twenties, much of my energy was spent on making sure men did not think I "needed" them, and that other women knew without a doubt that I would not give in to a man's desires over my own. Still, though self-sufficient and independent, I was in deep trouble, because under that facade I was a hopeless romantic.

I desperately tried to deny my romantic tendencies. I would tell myself I was living the life of my dreams, that I didn't "need" a man. But then those old familiar longings would unexpectedly surface, and at the most inopportune times: While at my favorite tea house, sipping contentedly on a cup of Earl Grey tea with a close girlfriend, I'd notice a young couple at a nearby table sharing affection, and I would feel envious. Or at home, I'd be engulfed in a new music project or writing up an idea for a seminar when sudden pangs of depression in my stomach would remind me I was alone again on a Saturday night. My longing for love grew, and yet I couldn't "find" it.

I knew, under my attempts to be a liberated woman, that there was something I didn't understand when it came to attracting men. In some arenas, I was an assured, expressive, articulate young lady, while in others I would revert back to being a timid girl. I had always been committed to personal growth and self-improvement, but inside I felt I was missing something. I wanted to embody the tender, joyful, radiant power I occasionally saw in other women. I felt stuck on a bridge between awkward adolescence and elegant, sensually alive womanhood, and I didn't know how to get to the other side. Eventually, rather than pretend to understand everything going on within me, I allowed myself to just be with my confusion. A wise friend had once told me that when you're confused, you're on the edge of a breakthrough. I hung onto her words, and sure enough, my discomfort and awkwardness ultimately led to an enormous transformation.

In 2002, I moved from Melbourne, Australia, the only home I had ever known, to Ashland, Oregon. It was time to reinvent myself. I felt liberated to be in a place where no one knew me, free to participate in whatever weird and wonderful experiences I cared to in this small tourist town full of affluent California transplants, well-off hippies, and people addicted to self-help workshops and retreats.

Just after my arrival in Ashland, a new friend offered me her ticket to a workshop she was unable to attend. "The focus of the weekend is on how to embody your feminine essence and how living in your own sexual essence positively affects your intimate relationships," she explained. *Feminine what? Sexual Essence??* Despite the nervous contractions in my stomach, my intuitive sense told me that this workshop would answer some of my biggest questions. I thought, *Might as well* and accepted the ticket.

The first morning of the workshop, I was greeted with an unexpected and very personal hug by a woman in her mid-thirties who, though clearly American, looked like she had just stepped out of a painting of an Indian Goddess. She pressed her lower belly up against mine for an uncomfortable moment, and, as we pulled apart, she grabbed my hands, opened her eyes as wide as she could, and stared deeply into mine. It felt like she was trying to say, "I am a deep and soulful person. Can you see that?" All I could see was that she was weird. She wore a long flowing skirt, was obviously not wearing a bra (the hug gave that away), and had a small blue jewel stuck between her eyes. My first thought was, *Oh My God! What if it's one of those women's workshops where you are given a hand-held mirror and a mat so you can comfortably rest back and gaze lovingly at your vagina while whispering sweet affirmations to it? Is it too late to creep out the side door?!*

Thankfully, she didn't have mirrors for us. However, I had never heard myself say, "You want me to do *what*?" so many times in one weekend. We were invited again and again to do some of the strangest things, all to get in touch with our own feminine energy. I had constant judgments about this "woo-woo" teacher who had been doing too much "energy work" for her own good and needed to return to Planet Earth. However, despite her "*woo-wooness*" and my own inner commentary, in the final hours of the weekend I touched on something I'll never forget—my authentic feminine essence.

In that moment of transformation, I felt myself shift internally from trying to be noticed as a strong, attractive woman to one who is seen as a source of radiant beauty and love that would fill any room. If you had been in the same room with me, you would have seen my physical body soften and relax as I felt my core strength build within me. I looked petite on the outside, but if you had tried to push me over I would have stayed solid as a rock, with little effort or resistance on my part. All my senses were heightened. My awareness expanded to the whole room rather than just what was in front of me. My movement became fluid, and I felt a huge amount of energy in my belly, hips, and pelvis. My physical power sank deeper into my body. Rather than feeling the need to puff my shoulders up to be strong, I felt like I was the base of an iceberg—vast, deep, stable, and secure.

Before this moment, I had been fearful of appearing too feminine or too sensual because I didn't want to have to deal with unwanted attention from men—what if they wanted something from me that I did not want to give? I was scared around females too—would they judge my self-love and self-expression as arrogance? But once I connected to my feminine essence, I felt safe to express all of who I was, no matter what anyone else might think. My "tough cookie" exterior that had been determined to have men understand that I did not "need" them began to melt away, and what replaced it was not submissive insecurity but a newfound powerful vulnerability that opened my heart.

That was the day I made it to the other side of the bridge, the day I fully embodied my feminine power.

THE FEMININE ESSENCE IS THE "E-SPOT"

The feminine essence lives inside every woman. The nickname I use for the feminine essence is the E-Spot—"E" because it's Energetic and so cannot be seen or physically felt like the G-Spot. An aroused G-Spot is nothing compared to the Ecstasy, Empowerment, and Effortless magnetism that are released when a woman activates her feminine essence. Your E-Spot is not only an attractive force within you, but it feeds you, feels soooo good, and is a gift that no one can ever take away from you. This book is about how to activate your feminine essence. It's my gift to you, and I'm excited to show you how to find the feminine essence within you—your own E-spot—and to turn it on and turn it up!

E FOR ENERGETIC

An essence is a dynamic quality that a person, place, or animal exudes. This essence is not something we can touch or scientifically measure, but we can all certainly feel it. Just as a dog has a different essence than a cow, a feminine person has a different essence than a masculine person.

We all have a distinct masculine essence and a distinct feminine essence within us, although the balance of masculine to feminine varies from person to person. When a woman activates her feminine essence, the energy that is in her body and around her moves differently than when she is in her masculine essence. This energy affects who we are attracted to, how we perceive each other, how we feel, and what we draw into our lives. Let's look at why the feminine essence is so attractive, and why it's attracted *to* the masculine essence.

We all know what happens when you point the opposite poles of a magnet towards each other: they snap together quickly. When like poles of a magnet face each other, they "push back," or repel. Now think of the "masculine" as the positive pole of a magnet and the "feminine" as the negative pole. Two people with the same sexual essence will generally not be as attracted to each other sexually; similarly, two people with the opposite sexual essence will tend to be more attracted to each other.

Since the dawn of the feminine movement, both men and women have rejected aspects of their respective masculinity and femininity in order to avoid being perceived as the macho caveman or the dependent helpless housewife. This was a dynamic that had been going on in my own life—I had disowned aspects of my femininity because I had feared that embracing them would make me weak and needy. I could also see this with many of my friends. It wasn't so much that we didn't put time into *looking* feminine, it was more about the masculine personas we projected so that we would appear strong and capable. On this continuum of masculine and feminine, the more "polarized" a couple is, the more sexual attraction they will experience. A very feminine woman, therefore, is likely to attract a very masculine man, and a woman who is just right of neutral on the chart below is more likely to attract a man who is also closer to neutral. This polarization is also present with homosexual couples; one person usually loves sharing more of their masculine and one more of their feminine. Seen this way, then, we can understand how it is that many women who walk around in "neutral" 90% of the day are not in a passionately alive relationship, even though they seem to have everything else going for them. When I thought about this, I realized I, too, hovered around the middle somewhere—not really masculine, but not feminine either. My personal magnetism was not nearly as strong as it could be because I had "neutralized" my feminine side.

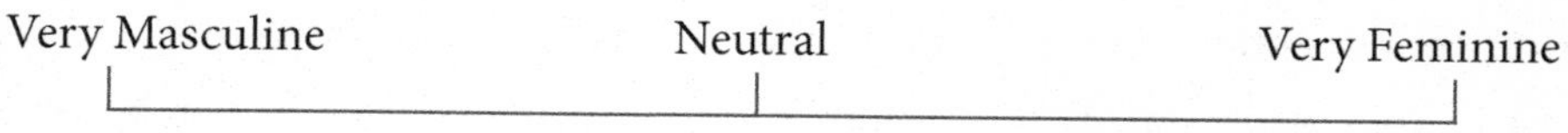

Very Masculine — Neutral — Very Feminine

I could see this happening in my love life. The men I attracted always tended to be the more neutral type. I called them "SNAGS"—Sensitive New Age Guys. I had thought they were the type of men I wanted—those more comfortable expressing emotion and their feminine side. However, what started out as attractive soon turned into disappointment. As my feminine essence began to surface in my relationships, I became bored when I was not met by masculine strength. I did not feel supported, and those relationships would inevitably end. However, as I started to use the exercises in this book and moved closer to the "very feminine" end of the spectrum, I found that I began to attract "very masculine" men.

Today, I am married and deeply in love with a strong, purposeful, healthy masculine man. I feel my real desires have been given permission to come forth. I have found myself surprised, confused, and sometimes even embarrassed by these deep, feminine desires, but I follow them rather than what I think I *should* do to fit the "feminist" mold. The self-sufficient and independent parts of me are still alive and well, as is the hopeless romantic in me, and all have made friends with the open, receptive, mysterious, and sensual parts that recognize I am interdependent with everything—whether I like it or not.

From my curiosity, study and practice with the feminine essence I created classes and trainings called *Art of Feminine Presence*. Little did I know how quickly this work would spread across the globe and how impactful it would be for my own personal and spiritual growth journey. The more I have practiced the work in this book and what I teach at the live trainings of *Art of Feminine Presence* the more unshakeable, powerful, safe, and joyful I feel.

E FOR ECSTATIC

When I am connected to my feminine essence, I feel relaxed, open, sensual, and alive. I feel sensations pulsing through my body that I never felt before.

In order to feel the ecstasy of your feminine essence, you must be able to shift your attention from your endless to-do lists to the one thing that's always "with" you: your body. When your attention is inside your body, you become present to the moment. When you drop down into the internal space of your body you start to attune to the sensations in your body; you become more open and receptive to the moment. As a rule, we are not raised to experience life this way. However, the more comfortable you become with feeling your body in the present moment, the more you will discover that it is inherently joyful, and, if you stay with it long enough, it becomes ecstatic.

THE MOST ATTRACTIVE FORCE WITHIN YOU

When I embody my feminine essence and I am in communication with someone else, I feel a warm feeling of connection in my body. And if another woman has her feminine essence turned on as well, the connection between the two of us is magical. Often, it brings tears to my eyes as I am so moved by the beauty in and around the woman in front of me. Activating your feminine essence increases the passion and ecstasy in your life, especially in your relationships. When you're in your feminine fullness, your magnetic charge is "turned on," and your ability to attract the attention and love you want will be ignited in the most delightful and effortless ways.

E FOR EMPOWERING

There are two primary ways to wield power—through assertion or attraction. As our society operates primarily in the more masculine way, many of us automatically use assertion over attraction.

If the power of assertion were represented in body language, you would see someone leaning forward, ready to reach out and take something. On the flip side, the power of attraction would be someone leaning back, ready to receive what comes to them, trusting that the energy they emit will attract what they want to them. Neither mode of power is better than the other. However, a person with a strong masculine essence is generally happier using their assertive power, while a person with a strong feminine essence is happier using their attractive power. Think of a dating scenario: Which gender typically enjoys pursuing a potential mate, and which enjoys attracting one?

When you are connected to your feminine essence and connected to the inner space of your body, the power of attraction is "on" and truly working for you. You generate a feeling of power within yourself no matter what is going on around you, and you do so without effort. Your feminine essence, then, is a great source of internal power. Many women don't feel safe as they start to attune to their feminine essence. Some share that they feel happier when they are neutralizing their feminine. What I observe in most of these instances is they are more comfortable living in their "masculine" or "neutral" essence because it's more comfortable and does not necessarily make them more alive and joyful. We often mistake comfort for true joy. I'll explain more about this in Chapter Three and how to move through the resistance to it.

E FOR EFFORTLESS

We all try to project personal qualities we want others to think we have; for example, we may want to be seen as sweet and friendly or smart and capable or confident and a force to be reckoned with. But when we project a forced sense of ourselves, we tire quickly. It's stressful. Not only that, but I will let you in on a little secret—almost everyone can see right through it!

Many women, in a misguided attempt to project more power, end up expressing primarily their masculine essence in both their work and social discourse. This rarely feels natural and can result in pushing others away. On the other hand, I find that both women and men are more responsive and respectful when I communicate with them from my feminine essence, and, because it feels more natural to me, I don't have to try so hard. When my feminine essence is alive in me, I feel like I don't need to force anything; I rely on my magnetic pull—and yet, at the same time, I know I have a strong masculine side and that I can be assertive if I need to be.

The feminine essence reminds us that life is a lot easier than most people live it. It offers us the invitation to soften our body, enjoy the moment, and trust the flow of life. We don't have to always push to make things happen. If you continue with the *Art of Feminine Presence* practices, you will find that you'll get more done in less time and be able to live the full vision you have for your life without getting burned out.

FEMININE BLESSINGS

It was my longing for love that propelled me into this beautiful world of learning and teaching the power of the feminine essence. In my work with now over twelve-thousand women, I have seen the following pattern over and over: A woman who doesn't embody her softness, her sensuality, and her feminine essence will stay confused, asking questions like "Where are all the good men?" and "Why do I feel something is missing?" She may find herself over-eating, over-shopping, or over-working to fill a hole that can never be filled. In contrast, a woman who embodies her feminine essence will have a better sense of herself and greater ease in creating lasting love, passion, and fulfillment.

Finding my own feminine essence was the missing key that finally unlocked the door and allowed love into my life. But romantic love, wonderful as it is, has only been one reward on a long list of benefits and blessings I have encountered on my journey with "the feminine." Since opening up to my own feminine essence, I have a newfound passion for people and life; I am doing the work I love; my purpose is clear and in harmony with who I am; and my relationships with women are less competitive and no longer full of comparisons. When I am connected to my feminine essence and walk into a room, I am noticed and acknowledged in a whole new way that complements and advances everything I do in my professional and personal life. My personal presence is stronger, and I am comfortable and at home in who I am.

Sadly, expressing our feminine essence is something many of us women have either forgotten or simply do not know how to do. This is through no fault of our own; we have not been taught how to be feminine in a healthy, centered, and powerful way. One of my goals is to help you to trust that consistently living in your feminine essence will lead you to life's greatest pleasures. Therefore, in this book I will guide you through some of the physical, emotional, energetic, and spiritual practices from the *Art of Feminine Presence* trainings that will amplify your own feminine essence and authentic power. A book is a great start to delve into this work before possibly joining me for one of our in-person intensives. (To find out more, visit **ArtofFemininePresence.com**.)

It is important to understand that a woman's journey to embody her feminine essence is not just for herself but for her family, her community, her country, and her planet. For centuries, we have distanced ourselves and our lives away from "the feminine." We have come to a point in history where the consequences of disowning "the feminine" are becoming apparent in painful, frightening ways: climate change, war, global economic crisis— as well as an overall lack of passion and purpose are just a few of the major costs. Women covertly pit themselves against other women in fierce competition for attention, men, career advancement, and "Mommy of the Year" awards. And far too many bright, self-sufficient women experience a lot of pain and disappointment in the area of relationships.

If you want to step out of this gloomy picture, if you want to create an extraordinary and fulfilling love relationship for yourself, if you want a passionate, purposeful, and peace-filled life, and if you want to feel confident, secure, and beautiful in who you are, then you must start to add "the feminine" back into your world.

You must make peace with and activate your feminine essence.

CHAPTER ONE SUMMARY

The feminine essence lives inside every woman. It is not only the most attractive force within you, but it feeds you, feels *so* good, and is a gift that no one can ever take away from you.

THE FEMININE ESSENCE IS THE E-SPOT:

- *E for Energetic*, because the feminine essence cannot be seen or physically felt like the G-Spot. It does, however, affect how you attract or repel others.
- *E for Ecstatic*, because the feminine essence feels relaxed, open, and sensual.
- *E For Empowering*, because when you are connected to your feminine essence, the power of attraction is "on" and truly working for you.
- ***E for Effortless***, because when my feminine essence is alive in me, I feel like I don't need to force anything but instead rely on my magnetic pull.

CHAPTER TWO

The Path to Wholeness

Wholeness is not achieved by cutting off a portion of one's being
but by integration of the contraries.

~ Carl Jung

For decades there has been controversy, misunderstanding, misinterpretations, revolts, blame, and lots of emotion centered around the word "feminine." What does "feminine" mean? Ask ten people and you are likely to get ten very different answers. Therein lies the problem. Then there are the broad categories, the "positive" and "negative" camps: some people want to bring the word "feminine" to the foreground of conversation and inspire more people to embody it, while others want it to go away saying it's irrelevant in this day and age, and that it just puts us in a box that no one should belong in.

We cannot progress further in our conversation here without addressing what I mean by the word "feminine" so it can be held in the context I've intended. I obviously believe exploring the feminine essence has a part to play in our cultural, personal, and spiritual evolution, but it's only one piece of the puzzle towards wholeness. Often people reduce the word "feminine" to gender or what the males in the culture think a woman should be like. On the other hand, some people use the word feminine and expand its meaning and all of a sudden feminine means so many things. Many people live within a reductionist mindset, and then project on to me that I'm trying to reduce "feminine" to a particular set of actions and beliefs or way of looking and speaking. That is far from what my message is about. I support women to find their own way of feeling and expressing their feminine essence.

I can empathize with why many people or groups reject the label of "feminine." In many ways those who disagree with me want exactly the same thing—for women to feel empowered and whole. We simply have different ideas of how to get there. The most common argument I hear is that we are neither masculine or feminine at the core of our being. We are spiritual and shouldn't be focused on our sexuality or gender. I agree that we are spiritual at our core. However, we are human beings having a spiritual experience. If we reduce ourselves to only focus on the spiritual part, the part of us that's forgotten or rejected plays havoc on us. We are physical as well as spiritual, so we must eat well and exercise to stay whole. Many self-proclaimed "spiritual people" are very unhealthy. We are also emotional as well as spiritual. I'm sure you've been around people who do what I call a "spiritual by-pass." This is where the "lower" human emotions are attempted to be ignored. Like the spiritual person who goes to church every Sunday and talks of love and forgiveness, but underneath the smiling façade lies a well of buried anger which comes out as passive-aggressive tendencies or an inappropriate outburst of anger and blame. Or like the "enlightened and evolved" spiritual person who considers themself an embodiment of love and light, yet acts towards others in thinly-veiled ego-based ways.

When I asked a few certified *Art of Feminine Presence* (AFP) teachers what concerns about the word "feminine" they were getting, here's some of what they shared with me:

"Some women believe that gender is not something we should even consider any more. That we need to accept that it's not about being either male, female, or any other identification. We are just people."

I agree. We *are* just people, but we have to include in our awareness that we're *also* animals. Each gender has a different brain and hormones that affect ways of thinking and reacting. One gender can give birth, and the other cannot.

One gender is generally physically bigger and stronger. Gender is irrelevant in conversations like "Who makes better leaders, a woman or a man?" But to completely throw out gender from the equation is a reductionist mindset and doesn't allow us to solve some of the deeper problems underlying gender, like violence against women.

"Some people say they want to move toward a place of 'integration' or 'wholeness,' beyond the feminine or masculine, instead of connecting more to their feminine, sexual essence."

I couldn't agree more. But wholeness comes not from denying aspects of ourselves, but from including more of who we are. Wholeness comes when we integrate our spiritual, physical, emotional, energetic, and sexual essence. The three levels of awareness I am about to share will shed more light on why integration is about including more of who we are, not moving beyond aspects of who we are.

"There are too many limitations about what 'feminine' is."

I agree with this as well. That's why it's important to go within and find out what it means for you and how can it bless your life, versus taking on someone else's small-minded definition.

"Some women reject the word feminine because they are aiming for equality in their life. Presence is the balance of both masculine & feminine qualities."

I feel this is another example of a reductionist mindset. As you'll read below, I experience "Presence" as a different level of awareness to the balance of yin and yang qualities or masculine and feminine qualities within me. Things that evolve become more complex organisms, not simpler. We need to integrate all parts of us that may be at different levels of awareness.

Another AFP teacher said this:

"My 17-year-old who identifies as non-binary says the beauty and joy of being non-binary means they can slide all around on the scale of masculine and feminine by the minute/hour/day/week."

To this I replied that I too can freely move in and out of my masculine or feminine essence throughout my day and my life. I don't call myself non-binary though. I see it as freedom to choose. We all have freedom to choose what feels more joyful and revitalizing in the moment.

These types of discussions that my team of teachers and I have been having with our communities is exactly why having clear definitions is important. I want to explain more about what I mean by "feminine" and how the feminine essence doesn't encompass all levels of awareness that are important in your growth. The feminine essence is only one part of the equation.

First of all, we work on three levels of awareness in *Art of Feminine Presence,* and all levels are important for every human to consider if we are to live a happy, functional life in a human body. This is a path to wholeness. If you try to transcend to a higher stage of awareness but deny the more human aspects of awareness without including them as you evolve you will create dysfunction. On your evolutionary path, if you transcend and include lower aspects of consciousness, you will move toward wholeness. Within each of these levels we work with the mind, body, and spirit because an integrated approach always accelerates wholeness rather than just working on one aspect of a human being.

The three levels of awareness that need to be integrated to experience wholeness are:

- Pure Consciousness (Presence)
- Yin and Yang Balance (Non-resistance)
- Primary Sexual Essence (Life Force)

PURE CONSCIOUSNESS (PRESENCE)

The "all that is" consciousness is everywhere, including within each of us. There is no boundary to it. It does not go away. It's not damageable. It's always present. It's the presence that permeates and animates everything.

Within and around the body we sense it as a refined, subtle presence that is not masculine, feminine, nor human in nature. People often connect with it through the subtle vertical core of their body. It radiates out to join with the "all that is" field. I sometimes call it "The Undeniable Matrix." It is pure consciousness or presence. Other names for it can be "Spirit," "Infinite Consciousness," "Higher Power," "Brahman," "God," "Allah," "Universal Intelligence," etc. During *Art of Feminine Presence* events and practices, we help women get in touch with this infinite consciousness as an embodied awareness, not just a concept they've heard about or studied.

YIN AND YANG BALANCE (NON-RESISTANCE)

We are spiritual beings having a human experience. Therefore, it's critical that we work with the issues of our humanness and the limitations of our mind, body, and energy if we are to become freer of the mental habits, emotional habits, and defense mechanisms that keep our ego (or protective personality) running the show. In the process of awakening it's important to realize that we are all aspects of nature. We are the yin and the yang. We are patient and impatient, cold and warm, receptive and directive, leaders and followers, fluid and rigid. Every aspect of our humanity serves a purpose. If we decide we want to be less reactive to others, we need to be non-resistant to every part within us, which means we need to fall in love with and integrate all parts of us; both dark and light. If the present moment calls for energies like anger and protest, we could bring them up and use them. If another moment called for energies such as stillness and patience, we could bring those forward and use them. When someone has a balance of yin and yang in their expression they are more whole, and interestingly have more magnetism. During *Art of Feminine Presence*, we help women integrate all parts of themselves so that they don't resist any one part. This lessens the hold of past memories and habitual ways of being, and supports them to realize themselves as pure consciousness in more moments. It supports them to be more present and not stuck in cultural overlays of what a feminine woman should be or act like.

PRIMARY SEXUAL ESSENCE (LIFE FORCE)

Our life force is intrinsically tied to the awakening process. Our sexuality is part of that life force. If we disconnect from our sexuality, we can easily create kinks in the hose of our life force, which can block us from feeling our presence and power. Many women—in the pursuit of equality with men, productivity in the workplace, or as a way to feel safer in the world—have shut down or misused their sexuality.

We all can access the masculine essence or feminine essence within us, but usually one is primary. When we fully access our primary sexual essence and let **it flow, we feel happier, more magnetic, healthier, sexier, and more connected** to the present moment. Many women don't realize that essence is shut down within them.

The feminine or masculine essence is not a spiritual part of us; it is the human sexuality part of us. This is not gender-based; this is sexual essence. If that gets denied, and the feminine is her primary sexual essence, challenges can occur in a woman's life. For example, if a woman's body runs a lot of masculine essence energy for a long time her body will burn out because most feminine bodies were not meant to run on masculine energy long-term. She may start to feel anger and resentment towards the world when her energy gets depleted and may become unwell physically and/or emotionally. During *Art of Feminine Presence*, we help women access this life force, and subsequently the healing, insight, and joy that arises when they allow more of their primary sexual essence to not be repressed or misused.

There is another level of awareness that needs to be taken into consideration, but we don't focus much on it in this work—that is gender. Just because you have the anatomy of a female, doesn't mean you should focus on your feminine essence primarily. Perhaps your primary sexual essence is masculine. You have the choice. It's important to separate gender (the physical gender and the cultural overlay of gender) with sexual essence (the energy of sexuality and life force).

We live in an era of various sexual-identity groups. Whether you align as transgendered, gay, heterosexual, bi-sexual, or something else, I believe this conversation relates to us all to some degree. In ten years of teaching this work, we have welcomed people representing all of these groups. Even though I cannot intimately understand all of the specific challenges faced by all specific orientations, I feel love for all of them. We have enjoyed many homosexual, transgendered, and bisexual women into this work and I pray that we are able to work with more over the coming years.

As humans, we're never going to agree on everything. We are all at different stages of conscious evolution and perceive things differently given our history, culture, groups we identify with, and stage of consciousness. The only way to stop fighting and judging others' beliefs is for more of us to realize and express our true nature as conscious, loving beings who are connected to everyone and everything.

I personally love the dance between all these levels of awareness. When I see people who are mostly outside their bodies focusing on their spiritual nature, they can be challenged with manifesting all they want in their life. When I see someone only trying to become a balance of masculine and feminine they are also challenged, and definitely when someone is focused on their sexual essence above everything else, their integrated power is not flowing through their life. Increasing your manifesting power requires integrating all three levels.

CHAPTER TWO SUMMARY

Wholeness comes not from denying aspects of ourselves, but from including more of who we are. Wholeness comes when we integrate our spiritual, physical, emotional, energetic, and sexual essence.

The three levels of awareness that need to be integrated to experience wholeness are:

- Pure Consciousness (Presence)
- Yin and Yang Balance (Non-resistance)
- Primary Sexual Essence (Life Force)

CHAPTER THREE

WHAT IS THE FEMININE ESSENCE?

Feminine power isn't something we go out and acquire;
it's already within us.
It's something we become willing to experience.
Something to admit we have.

~Marianne Williamson

When I mention to women, "I help ladies connect with their feminine essence," I often get comments like, "Oh I've been there and done that. I don't really care about dressing up and doing my makeup anymore, that's just not for me."

Being feminine is not about how much makeup or jewelry you wear, unless that leads to you feeling more beautiful and feminine inside. It's not about painted nails, long hair, how much pink you wear or how submissive you are. It has nothing to do with your choice of working in a corporate office or not, or of having babies and being a stay-at-home mom or not. It is, however, the most attractive force on the planet. It's what makes us glow. And, like every woman, we have constant access to it.

We all know that women are different from men. We have different brains, different bodies, different shapes, different hormones, different ways of communicating—and we have different sexual essences too. We all have a specific dynamic quality, or essence, to our personality, but the fundamental essence of a woman is quite different from that of a man. Although all humans have both a feminine and masculine essence within them, one of these is always primary. At her core nature, a woman feels much more pleasure when her feminine essence is primary, and a man when his masculine essence is primary.

Your feminine essence is activated when you make certain physical, energetic, and emotional shifts. In a moment, I will give you some practical and easy ways to experience your own feminine essence so that you can start to experience what it feels like for you—in your body, in your heart, and in what you become most present to. But first, let me answer a question I always get at the beginning of my seminars:

DOES EVERY WOMAN HAVE A FEMININE ESSENCE?

The answer is Yes! Every woman has a feminine essence, and every woman has access to it. Not only that, but most women's feminine essence is their primary sexual essence. In my experience, I see only approximately 5% of women where this is not the case (there is nothing wrong with these women; they simply feel more enjoyment when they are embodying and expressing their masculine essence). Although most women's feminine essence is their primary essence, many women energetically cover it up, like an old dusty sheet covering a beautiful piece of antique furniture.

The fact that you have picked up this book and are still reading it indicates you are most likely a woman whose feminine essence is her primary sexual essence—the question is how much, and whether you express it with confidence and joy.

THE YIN-YANG

It's often helpful to think in terms of yin and yang because it helps me move away from the idea that feminine means "woman" and masculine means "man." The theory of yin and yang, central to Taoism and Traditional Chinese Medicine, states that the world is made up of two opposing yet complementary forces—yin (feminine) and yang (masculine). In this philosophy, yin and yang work together to create harmony and order in our natural world. When these two qualities are out of balance, resistance and ultimately disease (dis-ease) result. A world where only the masculine or the feminine way of living is honored is not a world of harmony and does not lead us to where we want to go. Both yin and yang are integral pieces of the puzzle that create balance, passion, and sustainability.

YIN-YANG SYMBOL

When you look at the yin-yang symbol, you'll see that the yin side of the yin-yang symbol is black with a small white dot. The other side of the symbol is white with a small black dot—that is the yang side. This symbol was first created to show the phases of the seasons. The yin side represents the winter time, the time of the year with the least amount of sunlight. The yang side represents the summer time, the time of the year with the most amount of sunlight. The small dots represent the shortest and longest days of the year and remind us that within the dark there is always light and within the light there is always dark. Like the yin and yang in the symbol, each of us contains both feminine and masculine qualities within us; it is just a matter of degree how much we use them.

Listed below are some traditional continuums that represent the yin and the yang. The yin pole is receptive, watery, and represents the earth. It is the negative magnetic pole that works with attraction rather than assertion. The yang pole, on the other hand, is directive, fiery, and represents the sun. It is the positive magnetic pole that is actively creating.

TRADITIONAL YIN – YANG TABLE

Feminine – **Masculine**
Winter – Summer
Dark – Light
Passive – Active
Receptive – Directive
Soft – Hard
Downward – Upward
Cold – Hot
Water – Fire
Earth – Sky
Moon – Sun

Beyond the more traditional understanding of yin and yang, more interpretative aspects have been added over time. For example, according to the traditional understanding, yin is associated with winter and nighttime, and so the interpretative aspects of "internal" and "shadow" (qualities associated with winter and nighttime) may also be assumed:

INTERPRETATIVE YIN – YANG TABLE

Feminine **– Masculine**

Internal – External

Shadow – Transcendence

Mother Earth – Father Spirit

Nature – Culture

Feeling – Thinking

Intuition – Logic

Attraction – Assertion

Collective – Individual

Flexible – Rigid

Flow – Go

Process – Outcome

Sustainability – Peak Experience

Let's look at some of the aspects of yin and how they relate to a person who is embodying the feminine essence, and why people often equate "yin" to "feminine."

Yin represents the winter. I tend to hibernate in the colder months, and not do as much. Nights at home watching a movie are more frequent, and curling up to read a good book in front of the wood stove feels much more inspiring than braving the bitter cold nights in Northern Colorado. What I love about winter is that I feel a natural inclination to rest and become more introverted. When I am not as active, I have more opportunity to look within and reassess my life for the seasons to come. A woman who embodies her feminine essence is intimate with her internal experience. She often looks inward to her physical, emotional, and energetic body to guide her. She waits for the "right time" to make a choice or a change. Attuned to her intuition, she does not feel the need to rush ahead or struggle to achieve her goals.

The rhythm of the feminine is slower than the usual pace people move at. A woman in tune with her feminine essence is more in joy, flowing with the sensual beat of life, rather than always on the go, forging ahead. People tend to move slower in Hawaii, for example, where the feminine energy is very alive, than they do in downtown Chicago, where the environment is very masculine. This does not mean that a feminine woman can't move fast and be productive throughout her day. In some of the *Art of Feminine Presence* trainings, I have a group of women walk around the room as fast as they can without disconnecting from their feminine essence. If they can stay with the energy of their hips and heart, what happens when they get faster is that they get more powerful and magnetic. I'm always struck by how inspired I am by a woman who can be in her faster yang energy, while staying in her feminine. I often say, "These are the women I want leading our companies, communities, and countries."

Yin energy is expressed through feelings rather than thoughts. Both thoughts and feelings are important, but each plays a different role. Thoughts are linked to our minds' intelligence, whereas feelings are connected to our hearts' and bodies' intelligence. The feminine essence lives in harmony with emotions and energetic sensitivity rather than just with logic and strategy. If a woman in tune with her feminine essence wants to solve a problem or gain clarity on her next step in life, she uses her heart and body as her guide. She allows her feelings and desires to have a voice in her decisions rather than just following what she thinks is rational and what everyone else thinks she "should" do. Because she is attuned to her heart, she feels satisfied.

The feminine essence is not focused only on *doing* to accomplish and create what it wants, but it *understands the power of being*. What we are *being* is something that comes from within us, rather than something external we "do" to make something happen. In any moment of the day, we can choose to become aware of what we are being (am I *being* patient, loving, supportive, annoying, open, defensive, etc.) rather than simply being aware of what we are doing. "Being" is pure potential, like the egg waiting for the sperm to join with it to create an extraordinary masterpiece. Like the egg, a woman embodying her feminine essence does not have to control her environment to make something happen. She's much more in love with the process rather than achieving a fixed outcome, and so her power comes from a natural responsiveness and not a direct independent action. A woman in her feminine essence knows that, before she walks into any room, all she has to do is choose to feel her compassionate nature, her charm, her wit, her patience, or whatever the moment calls for, and it is with her. Her state of *being* automatically affects what comes out of her mouth, who and what she is drawn to, and what type of impression she leaves.

Yin is the receptive power. The feminine essence opens to receive, whether that be emotional support, insightful guidance, help getting things done around the house, or favors that can help her expand her business. Unfortunately, being a person that is open to receive is easier said than done, especially for most women. We have been conditioned to give, give, give, as if that were the way to be valued and loved: "If you give to your partner, give to your kids, give to your work, give to the household chores, give to the PTA, give to church, give to any friends in need—give to everyone except yourself—you will be a good woman."

There is much power in being open to receive. In fact, masculine men are much more drawn to women who love to receive their gifts, women who readily display that they have room in their life and a need for a partner. Think about this the next time you don't show gratitude to a man who wants to help you in some way. Instead you say, "I can do it myself." If your habit is to not accept or ask for support, you are cutting off one of the most attractive forces the feminine has. There are many examples of empowered women who allow men to support them; we will explore this in further depth later on in the book.

There is a nuance here that is important to recognize. Just because a woman is clear, direct, and at ease with leadership does not mean she is not feminine. Often, I have heard comments like, "She's in her masculine," just because a woman is being assertive and direct with something she says. This is not only unfair, but it is a diluted way to describe the feminine and masculine essences. A woman can express her yin qualities and still be an excellent communicator. She can be feminine and still know what she wants and how to get it. Given that magnetism is amplified when a human accesses both their yin and yang qualities, I often have to remind feminine essence women to befriend their authoritative and edgy side in order for them to be seen in the way they want. You can have it both ways. You can be powerful *and* feminine.

The feminine essence is the power of unity, connection, and relationship, which weaves all of creation together rather than just focusing on the individual. A woman living in her feminine essence longs to connect with what's around her. She wants relationship. She wants to love and be loved. I have a well-developed masculine essence—I love to lead and work hard in my business, and I enjoy life when I accomplish my goals. However, my deepest longing is for intimate communion. When I am honest with myself, I acknowledge that above everything else what my feminine heart wants is to connect with others in a deep and soulful way.

Yin represents the dark side. A woman in her authentic feminine power knows how important it is to look at the parts of herself that she keeps hidden in the dark. A question I often ask is, "What aspects of myself have I agreed to push into the shadows and not show others? Is it okay for me to be angry, selfish, competitive, or sad?" The more I integrate all the parts of myself (not just the helpful, friendly, nice, pleasing woman parts of me), the more I experience inner strength, freedom, and authenticity. The sexy, loving, wild, bitchy, dominating, compassionate, soft, and vulnerable parts all have a place within each of us. A powerful feminine woman understands this and honors all those parts. She also knows that to pretend our individual or global challenges do not exist, or to say, "Let's not focus on the problem," or, "Everything is perfect," is not only not helpful but keeps dysfunction in place. Sure, it's wonderful and effective to be a positive thinker and to focus on what you want for your world rather than what you don't, but sweeping things under the carpet helps no one. One of my good friends always says, "You can spray paint dog poop, but it does not make it go away."

The dark yin also represents the mysterious nature of the feminine. Humans are attracted to whatever they can't quite touch or figure out. We love enigmatic actors and models. Often, celebrities are asked to pose in a way that makes them look like they have a secret, or in a way that makes them look a little "bad-boy" or "bad-girl." The feminine essence is mysterious, and men love "unwrapping" this aspect of a woman to try to taste the mystery for themselves.

The feminine energy that runs through the body often feels watery. It's the soft, fluid, flexible, circular movement that we often feel in our hips and belly, not the tensed-up and stressed-out energy that runs through many women's bodies today.

Yin is the earth element. A woman in her feminine essence is in touch with the natural environment, with Mother Earth, with the tides and phases of the moon, and with her relationship to all animals. In our plight to move culture ahead as quickly as possible, we have almost entirely forgotten our partner, Mother Earth. In the Western World, we have been stuck in the idea that the world revolves around us, but the belief that everything in nature is for our benefit, consumption, or amusement is finally catching up with us. We have created physical disease and environmental devastation in more ways than most of us are willing to admit. In our times of greatest strife and challenge, we tend to look upwards to our Father in Heaven to help us and direct us, but we can also look downwards to another guide that is equally as powerful and wise—Mother Earth.

I love swimming in the soft—and sometimes wild—sensual pool of my femininity. This week alone, I enjoyed dancing, talking with friends, journaling, and other activities that I didn't feel had to lead to an end outcome. I felt all of my emotions fully, from excitement to frustration to sadness to ecstasy—all of which helped me get clear on what I *really* want. I appreciated the new ideas and inspirations that seemed to come from nowhere. I found new and relatively easy ways I can reduce my consumption of the world's resources and do my part to honor Mother Earth. I cherished feeling my partner's love rush up and through my body, which reminded me that I don't need to *do* anything to be loved except *be* present, vulnerable, and expressive in a way that feels good to me. I enjoyed supporting him in his direction and purpose while staying true to my own visions of running a business from a feminine perspective, one that adds to the world rather than takes from it.

If you've ever surrendered to witnessing a brilliant piece of art, you have undoubtedly been changed by it. Its color, beauty, and expression left an imprint not just on the canvas but on your soul as well. The life of a feminine woman is like that stunning work of art. The way she speaks, eats, moves, loves, and prays is an offering to life and whoever chooses to witness it, and the person who truly sees her is forever changed.

EXERCISE #1

Think of some women who embody a strong feminine essence (whether you know them personally or not). What qualities do you notice about these women that are different from other women?

Journal Question: *How do you feel about your own feminine essence?*

Before we jump into practical, specific ways you can activate your own feminine essence, it's important to recognize why you turned it off—or at least turned it down—to begin with. By looking at the negative messages and untrue stories that have been told over the years about the qualities of the feminine, we can acknowledge them, forgive them, and choose a different story. It is time for women to express all of their feminine juiciness, no matter what anyone else has to say about it. It is time for a new story.

CHAPTER THREE SUMMARY

The feminine essence is a dynamic quality that moves inside every woman. We all have constant access to this essence.

THE "FEMININE ESSENCE" IN A WOMAN IS:

- Attuned to her intuition and internal guidance
- Comfortable in the flow of life and moving slower than the fast pace around her
- Expressive of her feelings and heart's desires
- Aware of who she is when she walks into a room
- Receptive and attractive
- Connected to her longing for relationships
- Not afraid of her dark side (her shadow)
- Mysterious
- In touch with the earth and her impact on the natural environment

CHAPTER FOUR

"Nice Girls Don't" and Other Cultural Taboos

We will discover the nature of our particular genius
when we stop trying to conform to our own
or to other peoples' models,
learn to be ourselves,
and allow our natural channel to open.

~Shakti Gawain

Today, it is more perplexing than ever to determine how a woman should act, in the boardroom, in the bedroom, on the dating scene, or if she wants to become the next president. How she was encouraged to behave in these arenas just 10 years ago (let alone 50 or 60) was quite different than today.

There is much to be grateful for as we look back at the courage and victories of the previous waves of the women's movement. It cannot be denied that we have made many positive steps towards allowing women more power. However, in the pursuit of that power, many women have taken on a more masculine role without realizing it. Many of us women have no idea anymore of the pleasure and power that are released when we activate our feminine essence because our culture has sent negative messages such as "it's not needed," "it will bring you negative attention," and "if you use it too much, it will hold you back."

There are four primary messages that have caused women to shy away from the full expression and enjoyment of their feminine essence:

NEGATIVE MESSAGE #1: "The masculine is more productive and gets the job done!"

Whether you believe the glass ceiling for women in business is a perceived concept or a very real challenge that women face, I have heard time and time again that when a woman enters a man's world she is expected to act more like a man. We women have been told that placing more importance on furthering our careers over fostering our relationships, making our workspace more effective for production over making it look and feel beautiful, and holding tunnel-vision focus on the outcome of a situation over the rewarding process of getting there will lead to more success. In essence, the message has been, "the masculine is more productive and gets the job done!"

As a result of this mindset, many women believe that if they sink too deep into their feminine essence they will miss out on success. But that has not been my experience. When I am in my feminine, it is easier to be present in the moment and feel more joy and spaciousness, and therefore I get more done when I choose to be productive. I feel less stress, and my appetite for life increases. My desires are clearer and greater in number. I feel more alive, awakened, and motivated to follow through on what I want. When I do *not* connect to my feminine essence, I feel less spark for life and less in tune with myself or anything that is around me. It's as though everything were in black and white. Then, when I re-engage with my feminine essence, everything comes back into bright color and high definition. Sadly, most women and men move through their days in black and white, disconnected from the vibrancy in their own life because they are disconnected from their own sexual essence.

NEGATIVE MESSAGE #2: "Feminine is weaker than masculine."

Another message that we hear frequently, although in a more disguised form, is, "Feminine means weak." Have you ever judged a very feminine woman as weak, superficial, or ditzy? Have you ever dismissed your own desire to be more feminine after judging it "less than" in some way? As a general rule, women are more emotional, physically softer, more beautiful, and place higher priority on relationships than men. These are wonderful qualities but are also why people often view the feminine as weaker and less powerful than the masculine.

My clients who work in male dominated environments often are convinced they have to be fully in their masculine to "match it with the men." But a woman will never "out-male" a man who is in his power. If she can disengage from this artificially projected masculine strength and start to feel her feminine power, she will start to feel her true equality with the men around her.

This doesn't mean she won't use her masculine qualities to get things done, but she will balance this with the grounded, attractive quality of her feminine essence.

When a woman starts to disengage from her masculine essence, she may not feel powerful at first. This is not because the feminine is weaker, it's because she doesn't know how to embody and harness this other power quite yet. It is a process that takes some practice. This process reminds me of when my tennis coach told me to change the way I gripped my racket. I didn't want to let go of the grip I was used to because I could already hit the ball strong enough, and with the newer grip I went backwards. But, with practice and patience, I eventually learned the new grip and ended up with a stronger, more accurate swing than I had ever had with the old one. Re-engaging your feminine essence is a process. Be patient with yourself through this change.

I am grateful that studies in leadership and business management are now reporting that high levels of "Emotional Intelligence" are what distinguish both effective corporate leaders and managers as well as moms and social workers. Women are now in fulfilling careers that were previously just for males. I am inspired when I attend meetings where millions of dollars are raised to help those less fortunate—all because a group of women worked together for a common cause. The feminine is anything but weak.

NEGATIVE MESSAGE #3: "It's not safe to be feminine."

Some women have suffered through traumatic experiences that have left them with the overwhelming message, "it's not safe to be feminine." Direct or second-hand experiences of rape, childhood sexual abuse, and/or attracting unwanted sexual attention have enormous implications on how a woman relates to her feminine essence. After any of these horrific events, a woman may put on weight, drastically lose weight, or not put much attention on feeling sexy, beautiful, and feminine. She may link her own feminine sexuality with being hurt, betrayed, and controlled. As a result, most women feel uncomfortable with unwanted attention from men, even if it is a harmless stare at their beauty.

You don't have to look far to see countless cases of violence against women. We can also be influenced by less traumatic situations; like being told by parents that we shouldn't be too "girly" or too sexy. It's easy to start taking on other people's fears.

To be safe in this world, a woman must claim her power, especially her sexual power. When a woman does not own her sexuality in a wholesome way she opens herself up to be taken advantage of. The exercises in this book will show you ways to keep strong, healthy boundaries without dimming your radiant Light, and to feel your unshakable power no matter what wanted—or unwanted—attention comes your way. If you continue to practice this work you will find yourself feeling truly safe in your own skin and safe to take the spotlight when you feel called to do so.

NEGATIVE MESSAGE #4: "It's politically incorrect to be too feminine."

We constantly adapt to our environment, which is how we survive. I was never told blatantly "you need to act like a man;" it was just something that happened as I adapted to my environment. I remember Annie Lennox and Aretha Franklin singing, "Sisters are doing it for themselves," followed by Alanis Morissette dominating the charts, screaming angry songs that were in no way feminine. I looked around me and saw that being logical and driven would lead me to more success than being an "emotional" woman would. I heard from the leaders of the women's movement that we could get farther taking on more masculine traits. I didn't look for my feminine essence because I didn't have any reason to. If I had found it earlier than I did, I probably wouldn't have known what to do with it anyway—I didn't know how to live in this culture without my masculine essence "out front" to help me get ahead.

There seem to be two main groups that young women fall into during their formative years in high school and college: Those who are "pro-culture" and those who are "counter-culture." The pro-culture group is obsessed with following the latest advice and trends in the magazines that tell them they have to be beautiful like celebrities. They want boys to want them and will do almost anything to get that attention. The "counter-culture" group is the young women who have moved from the pro-culture way of life to the other extreme, attempting to make a loud statement of "I don't care how I look," "I don't care about male attention," and that it is politically incorrect to be "too feminine."

We swing away from the feminine in us as mature women as well. When we see images of women who use their femininity in manipulative ways, or when the pornography industry propagates a distorted and disgusting image of feminine sexuality, it can make those of us that want to be taken seriously run in the opposite direction. Many women move away from their feminine essence because it doesn't seem to be the path to being a person who is truly respected, listened to, and seen as powerful. This is what we have been taught in the last few decades; in the 70's, 80's, and 90's, it was politically correct to be a more masculine woman who didn't need any help from any man. Thankfully, the pendulum is now swinging in the other direction, and women are once again embracing the concept that it is possible to be both powerful *and* feminine.

YOUR DEFINITION OF FEMININE POWER

How we are told a powerful woman should look and behave will continue to change as culture changes. Confusion and dissatisfaction will increase until we support each other in defining for ourselves what a powerful woman looks like. The question, "how do I want to express myself as a woman?" has to replace the relentless statement—backed by billions of dollars in advertising and political campaigns—"this is how you *SHOULD* want to express yourself as a woman."

Instead of continuing to follow all the outside messages, let us go within to ask, and then answer, this fundamental question:

Does my current definition of a powerful woman serve me?

Look at your existing beliefs about femininity, having children, being ambitious, placing attention on beauty, or being loud and strong. Do they serve you? Do you sometimes try to live up to an image that doesn't really fit you? Do you sometimes try to follow what others say will lead to happiness when deep down you know that path won't satisfy your soul? Do you sometimes forget to breathe and relax during your day because your dominant belief is that you have to push yourself to be successful? These are not simple questions to answer, but it's time to take a good look at them.

Freedom to embody your own authentic expression of femininity is possible when you become aware of what you have been taught it means to be feminine and womanly. To re-engage with the feminine within you, you will need to get around these fairytales so you can go deeper within yourself and enjoy your own feminine essence. Every woman has a unique feminine expression. Discover yours, and then express it fully, without apology. It will feel delicious to you, and the result will be your own personal work of art, a work of art like no other.

EXERCISE #2

Take an inventory of the beliefs you hold about what being feminine and womanly means. Do you believe a woman's destiny is to have a child and that if she doesn't, she's missing out on a woman's greatest role? Do you believe a woman is a failure if she never marries? Do you believe that women are the world's greatest hope and that men have messed up our society? Keep asking yourself this question, "What do I believe being feminine and womanly means?" Don't judge your answers, just notice what you think and believe.

Here are some beliefs from my own list before I started practicing the *Art of Feminine Presence* work I now teach:

1. You have to be beautiful to be noticed.
2. It's not ladylike to be bossy or loud.
3. You have to always be polite and accommodate others.
4. Women have to work harder than men to get to the top of a company.

Write down your beliefs in your journal or Feminine Guidebook

It's time to activate our feminine essence and understand how to use it for good. Remember, no feminine essence looks the same, sounds the same, or feels the same. Yours will express itself in its own beautiful and unique way. However, there are some consistent variables to the feminine essence that you should first be aware of. Let's start by exploring what the feminine essence actually feels like in your body and then discover the quickest way to turn it on.

CHAPTER FOUR SUMMARY

Many of us have no idea of the pleasure and power that are unlocked when we find our feminine essence because our culture has repeatedly sent such negative messages as, "It's not needed," "It will bring you negative attention," and "If you use it too much, it will hold you back."

Negative message #1: "The masculine is more productive and gets the job done!"

Negative message #2: "Feminine is weaker than masculine."

Negative message #3: "It's not safe to be feminine."

Negative message #4: "It's politically incorrect to be too feminine."

Continue to look at your beliefs about femininity and what it means to be womanly. Question and challenge those beliefs. Make sure they empower you.

CHAPTER FIVE

The Quickest Way to Turn It On!

Attraction is beyond our will or ideas sometimes.

~Juliette Binoche

If you want to change the way you feel, change the way you move. If you want to change the way others feel about you, change the way you move. Look around you—it's not hard to tell who the most confident people in the room are, or the most depressed, or the happiest. You can see it without hearing a word or knowing anything about them. It's in their body language, their facial expressions, their posture—and in the way they move.

Before I walk into a room, I can choose to feel a certain way, and the quickest way to do this is to move. I can hold my head a little higher, open my shoulders a little wider, and breathe a little deeper. Without changing what I think, I feel different. When I become more deliberate and choose how I use my body, I am more able to make the positive impression I want to make. Physical movement is the most powerful and immediate way to change an emotional or energetic "state" and reach the levels of success we want. It also happens to be the quickest way to turn on your feminine essence.

If you want to activate your feminine essence and feel centered, receptive, and attractive to the masculine, there are ways you can move that are radically different from those you would use if you wanted to activate your masculine essence. Let's explore these movements so you can start to become aware of how alive it feels when you move with your feminine essence.

MOVING

When a movement is more masculine, the parts of the body that are primarily activated are the shoulders and upper body. Gestures tend to be hard, rigid and directive, not soft and fluid. When you are in your masculine mode, your "inner boxer" often comes out. You feel the most constriction or power through your upper chest (above your heart), your shoulders, and down through your arms. Have you ever seen two guys have a friendly fist fight? They look like they are enjoying it, don't they? They are! Or have you ever seen a passionate male sports fan at a football game? Fists punch the air in all directions—in jubilation, in irritation and in making sure the referees know how he feels. The energy in his body is moving in a masculine way, which inherently feels great to him.

Whenever I ask an audience of women to stand and exaggerate their masculine essence, I witness a sea of chests puff out and more energy move through their shoulders and arms. Her head looks straight on as she glares into the space directly in front of her, and she is equally weighted on both legs. Some women have even shared they feel like Popeye. I see a different vision when I ask a woman to stand and exaggerate her feminine essence. I see her take on a more flexible and non-symmetrical stance, with more of her energy in her hips and legs. Often, she will spontaneously start to sway from side to side. This is because the feminine energy feels watery and fluid in the hips and pelvis and down through the legs.

In my presentations on the feminine essence, I usually ask a volunteer to come to the front of the room and face the audience. With a few whispers in her ear, I guide her through the three instructions I am about to give you. Like magic, her feminine energy lights up the room, and her personal presence magnifies in an instant. Often, I hear an audible "wow" from the women, who, at this point, will do almost anything to find out what I whispered to her. I then share with them, as I am about to do with you, the three Feminine Activation Points, which are:

1. Rest your attention in the center point of your pelvis, your "womb space," and down your legs
2. Activate the sensual energy in your hips with movement
3. Soften your heart and allow your love to shine

Want to try it?

First, sit up straight, or stand, and bring your awareness down to your hips and pelvic area. Direct your attention to the center point of your pelvis, or womb space, which is approximately four inches below the navel and in the center of your body. Imagine a globe of light there. Focus on that light, and feel your legs connect to the earth. To do this, I often imagine my legs as tree trunks and that I have roots under my feet that sink into the ground at least fifteen feet. As you do this, you will feel more solid and powerful in the lower half of your body. To the audience, this makes a woman appear strong and centered.

Secondly, start to *slowly* isolate and move your hips in any way that feels good to you—from side to side, or in circles. This will activate your feminine essence. You will instantly feel pleasure in this simple movement. There may be other times when you want to turn this activation point on but are not in a situation where sensual hip movements are appropriate. In those cases, simply take a different stance and shift your weight to one side by bending one knee and putting one hip out a little—you don't always need to stand with your whole body symmetrical, like a man who is ready to tackle something. As you shift your weight to one side and back again, this engages the hips and pelvis, which is where the feminine energy loves to move. Try this first without a mirror to feel what it feels like internally to you, and then use a mirror to see the visual effect it has. The next time you want to turn on your feminine essence, simply shift your stance to one side. When I am with a volunteer, this is the activation point that is most noticeable to the audience; she starts to not only look strong and centered but also sensual and playful.

The final Feminine Activation Point is to soften and rest in your heart, and let love shine outward from there. Remain grounded, with the energy activated in your hips, and take some deep cleansing breaths. As you do, soften your heart as much as you can. Imagine there is a loving light coming from your heart, which is effortlessly beaming out into the room. If someone is there with you, look at them as if they were the most beautiful thing you have ever seen and send them love from your softened heart. When a man and woman make love, the man penetrates the woman with his penis to open the woman's vagina. This is energetically important on two levels. A woman's vagina is often the most guarded part of her body, and the man helps her open it with each loving thrust. The energy then moves up the woman's body to her heart, and she penetrates his heart with her heart. Likewise, a man's heart is often the most guarded part of his body, and the woman helps him open it with each loving beam of light she sends. His energy is then freer as it moves down his body, and the cycle continues. Sexual intercourse is a beautiful illustration of this exchange of heart energy, but you don't need to wait for a sexual embrace to open those around you with the soft strength of your heart penetrating theirs. Send that loving beam from your heart to anyone; it opens you as the giver and them as the receiver.

When the feminine essence is activated, the lower body is more weighted and connected to the earth, and the upper body is relaxed and soft. Be aware of any tightness in your neck and shoulders; this can be a sign that you have a lot of masculine energy moving inside you. Release it by relaxing your upper body as much as you can throughout the day.

By the time I have taken the above-mentioned volunteer through all three Feminine Activation Points, she not only looks strong, centered, sensual, and playful, she also feels loving and safe to be around. *That* is a magnetic woman, and that is the power of the feminine essence.

BREATHING

Your breath is your most fundamental movement. It is an instant way to activate your feminine essence and become present to the moment. We know that the feminine essence is activated through the belly, hips, and pelvis—practice taking a breath that drops low into this region. As you take a breath, invite the top part of your body to relax and soften. I invite you to practice this now by breathing in and out through your nose. On your first few breaths, become aware of your hips, belly, and pelvis becoming full and awakened. When you breathe in, your belly will expand as it fills with air, and when you breathe out, your belly muscles will contract as they squeeze the air out. Keep your attention on your belly muscles as you continue to breathe.

On your next few breaths, soften your shoulder area, and let go of any tension there. On the next few breaths after that, soften your heart area, and let go of any tension there. On your next few breaths, soften your throat and relax your jaw and face. In as many moments as you can, drop your awareness to your lower body and soften your upper body. This keeps your feminine essence engaged.

WALKING

It's hard to miss the fact that women and men walk differently. Women naturally swing their hips more and don't walk as fast as men. There is a flow and grace to a feminine woman's walk and a directive, strident nature to a man's. If you walked down New York's Wall Street, you may not see as much difference between the sexes because most of the women there work all day with their masculine essence out in front of them. Similarly, if you walked down a peaceful beach on Fiji you might not see as much difference between the men and women there because the men tend to be more comfortable with their feminine essence there. If you want to activate your feminine essence, learn to walk with it.

When a woman walks with her feminine essence, her center of gravity and attention is lower in her body: It's in her hips and belly, and the energy moves down her legs. When a woman walks with her feminine essence, she walks at her own pace while enjoying the sensations in her body. Her upper body is relaxed. She is aware of what is going on behind her as well as in front of her. When a woman walks with her masculine essence, on the other hand, she is generally only aware of what is directly in front of her—her awareness of her entire environment is cut off.

John Gray, in his book, *Men, Women, and Relationships*, explains this concept as the feminine being "open awareness" and the masculine "focused awareness." I usually can and will size up a whole room, from how it feels to what it looks like to who is there, before I choose where I will move and stand in that room. When I have women walk with their masculine essence and ask them to notice what they become aware of in the room, the answer is usually "not much, except what is directly in front of me." But when I ask them the same thing when they are in their feminine essence, the answer is usually "almost everything."

I used to set a daily time to consciously practice my feminine walk. Each morning, once I arrived at work, I would get out of my car and say to myself, "I am going to walk from this car to my office in the most feminine and pleasurable way I can." By the time I would get to my office, I would feel great and present to all that was around me. It was a much better "morning high" than a cup of coffee, and the added benefit was that people would notice me more. Often, I was told in the morning, "you look so great!" or, "you look so radiant this morning!" It wasn't about my clothes or whether I was having a good hair day; it was what my feminine walk invoked in me that radiated through my body and lit up the room. Don't waste another minute where you could enjoy your own feminine essence and at the same time light up someone else's day with your radiance! You can invite it in whenever you choose, when you stand in line, while you walk through the supermarket, or while alone at home as you make yourself a cup of tea. Take time to practice feminine movement, breathing, and walking, and notice how the world responds!

If you are like some of my clients who work in very fast paced, male-dominated workplaces or perhaps face "life-and-death" situations at work, you may be thinking "that's easy for you to say." I have a client—let's call her Mary—who works in a hospital and was initially very resistant to walking in her feminine at work. "I have to get so many things done at work, neither I nor my patients can afford for me to walk around 'all feminine' all day," she would say. It's true that in some workplaces it is more challenging to be in your feminine, but *take note*: To walk with your feminine essence does not mean that you have to walk slowly, swing your hips from side to side in a sensual way, or not care about getting where you are going on time. That is merely an elementary version of what the full feminine essence is. The feminine essence also has a strong, authoritative nature to it: it will protect, it cares deeply, and it will not allow anything to go wrong on its watch. I can both walk fast and be "on a mission" and still be connected to my legs, hips, belly, and surrounding environment. So, if you find yourself in a place where the soft, sensuous feminine is not appropriate, think of the strong, grounded feminine that doesn't need to push things out of her way but rather creates waves as she purposefully moves through the room with ease.

EXERCISE #3

Stand up and become "present" to your body. Bring to mind a color that represents a neutral state—not connected to any sexual essence. ***Then, bring to mind a*** *garment that feels very neutral to you—not at all masculine or feminine. If you were to put this garment on, you would feel very asexual. Now imagine this garment infused with the neutral color you thought of previously, and once you have it clear, start to put it on in your mind. As you do, imagine all masculine and feminine energy draining out through your toes. When you feel like you are in a neutral state (not connected to any sexual essence), start to walk around the room. Notice what you feel—physically, emotionally and energetically.*

Now you will walk with a masculine essence. To do this, bring to mind a color that represents the masculine state for you. ***Then, bring to mind a garment*** *that feels very masculine to you. If you were to put this garment on, you would feel very masculine. Now imagine this garment infused with the color you thought of previously, and, once you have it clear, start to "put it on." As you do, imagine all neutral and feminine energy draining out through your toes and* ***being filled with 100% masculine energy.*** *Now, walk with a masculine essence, with your attention in your upper chest and shoulders. Notice what you feel—physically, emotionally, and energetically.*

Finally, bring to mind a color that represents the feminine state. Next, think of a garment that feels very feminine to you. If you were to put this garment on, you would feel very feminine. Imagine this garment infused with the color you thought of previously, and, once you are ready, start to "put it on." As you do, imagine all neutral and masculine energy draining out through your toes ***and being filled with 100% feminine energy.*** *Now, walk with your feminine essence, with attention to your hips and your lower belly, and with a grace that comes with not needing to be anywhere or do anything. Notice what you feel—physically, emotionally, and energetically.*

Which mode felt more enjoyable and natural? What are the differences in where your attention went in the room with each mode? This week, pay attention *to the way you walk most of the time. Does your walk feel more masculine, more feminine, or neutral to you?*

Note: Some women choose to work with me because they think they are in their masculine energy most of the time and need to shift from masculine to feminine. What we discover together, however, is that they are actually in a neutral state most of the time; it is the shift from neutral (not connected to any sexual essence) to feminine that they need to explore the most. Which one is it for you?

SUBTLE MOVEMENT AND DANCE

When I add physical exercise into my daily routine, I see other areas of my life improve besides my health. My meditations are clearer, and my appreciation for life is easier to access. I am happier when all those endorphins flow through my body. Exercise is also important for creating beauty and radiance; we look better when we exercise. Both cardiovascular exercise and weightbearing exercise are essential. If you don't have a routine already, find one that works for you: Walking, cycling, weight lifting, a team sport, dance, yoga, swimming, etc.

I do have one word of caution, however. If you are a woman who often does rigorous, competitive, and tough sports, feeling the feminine essence through other types of movement is recommended—you must counteract the effect that comes when you move with so much masculine energy. That goes from the way you exercise to the way you work during the day. If you work in a masculine-dominated office all day, for example, you must add activities into your life that call forth the feminine in you, otherwise you will dry up. You will become less fulfilled, less vibrant, less juicy, and more stressed. When I want help to access my feminine essence, there are two activities at the top of my list that have added a great deal of pleasure to my life. They are:

1) Subtle movement, and 2) Dance.

Subtle Movement

There is an inherent internal pleasure that arises when you slow your movement down. One of the reasons for this is that when you slow down you can start to feel the movement of energy inside you. Some call this our subtle energy body, others our inner energetic body. If you place attention inside your hands right now, you may notice some sensations, perhaps a tingling or a buzzing. Energy is moving there, just as it is throughout your entire body, and when you move your physical body in slow, subtle ways and activate awareness of this subtle energy body, your joy levels rise and you become very present and "in the moment."

In my seminars, I ask the women present to move their body in a few subtle ways, like slowly moving their hands in front of their body as if they were two kites playing in the wind. My invitation to them is not just to watch their physical hands move but to put their attention on the subtle energy in their hands with the intention of enjoying it like they've never enjoyed moving their hands before. If you were in the room with me when they did this, you would see the corners of their mouths start to curl up. Their sense of enjoyment increases tenfold when they slow down the pace and increase the subtlety of their movement. A woman's body is built for subtlety and slowing down. After all, what is the biggest complaint women have of men in bed? SLOW DOWN!

Practice slowing down your simplest movement. Be present in your body and play a game with yourself as you ask, "How much can I enjoy this movement? How much can I enjoy brushing my hand through my hair? Can I get 'turned on' by touching my fingers together?" Focus on enjoyment and being inside your body rather than hovering "just above your forehead," worrying about all the things you have to do. Magic happens when your energetic body engages with your physical body. You feel lighter, and at the same time you become more visible. Your personal presence is palpable. You start to glow.

Dance

Dance, to me, is a powerful feminine form of meditation. One purpose of meditation is to still the mind and become present to the moment; the same is true of dance. It stills my mind and brings me more into the moment, but instead of energetically emptying myself to feel a sense of nothingness, I energetically fill up. Dance gets me in my body. It drops me down to my hips and belly; therefore, it is another way to access my feminine essence. This is why belly dancing and pole dancing classes have surged in popularity. Women report feeling empowered after these classes, not because they want to emulate the life of a stripper, but because their feminine essence is activated. Your dance could be swing, tap, tango, salsa, belly-dancing, pole-dancing, free-form, ballroom, or whatever takes your fancy—just choose one (or more). I personally love anything that is slow. I love moving underneath the beat.

Few of us move with total flow and freedom, without constriction or inhibition. Dance supports us to feel more flow. When we unlock our body, we unlock our self-consciousness. When we move in new ways, our minds are freed to think in new ways. I almost always know immediately which women are going to be the most resistant to enjoying their feminine essence by the way they move to slow music. If a woman's body is restrained, without much ease and flow, enjoying her feminine essence will be difficult for her. It is for this reason that I use movement as an integral part of my work. I love to support women to move in ways they have never moved before, as this will open their lives in ways they have never opened before.

EXERCISE #4

Put on some music that you don't usually listen to that has a sensual, uplifting beat. For at least five minutes, move to this music in a way you have never moved before. Isolate areas of your body that you may not normally move much. As you move, ask yourself these questions. "How can I move my arms in a way I have never moved them before?" "How can I move my torso in a way I have never moved it before?" "How can I move my head in a way I have never moved it before?" Have fun with this

An empowered feminine essence woman has a strong sense of physicality and wants to experience life through her body. Don't waste any opportunity you have to inspire others with your movement and your sensuality. It does not take a lot. Take time to move for enjoyment, slow down your walk, and dance, feeling the voluptuousness of your hips. All these things bring you more in tune with your surroundings, with the present moment, and with your masculine partner—who will be begging to come in and play.

CHAPTER FIVE SUMMARY

Focus on your physical movement when you want to turn on your feminine essence. There are both feminine and masculine ways to move. The feminine energy primarily moves in the hips and pelvis and down the legs. It feels watery and fluid.

THE THREE FEMININE ACTIVATION POINTS ARE:

1. Rest your attention in the center point of your "womb space" and down your legs;
2. Activate the sensual energy in your hips with movement; and
3. Soften your heart and allow your love to shine.

Breathe down into the lower belly as you soften your shoulders, heart, and throat.

Walk with your attention in the lower half of your body. Feel your legs connect to the earth, and move at your own pace as you enjoy the sensations in your body. Take up a practice that supports you in staying connected to the flow in your body.

CHAPTER SIX

Womb Wisdom

Every born leader—whether in the sphere of politics, great enterprises or the spiritual life—draws their strength from the primordial forces of life.

~Karlfried Graf Dürckheim

There is a part of a woman's body that is not given much positive attention, and that is her sexual organs. Most women do not inhabit the lower half of their body and dissociate with their sexuality. One area we particularly focus on in our *Art of Feminine Presence* trainings is what we call the "womb space." Our womb space is fundamental to unlocking our feminine energy, our ability to feel ecstatic moments often, and a sense of taking up our rightful space and being empowered. It is the place we create life from. It reminds us of the cycles of life month after month, for most of our life. It gives us strong feelings of intuition that are related to our survival and communication with others. In short, it is a powerhouse. However, this powerhouse has been diminished by our culture, which doesn't understand the wisdom that resides there. It has been diminished with the contraceptive pill, with hasty hysterectomies, and with misinformation about what this extraordinary organ can do. It's time now to take back that power, and to learn how to feel and follow the wisdom of our womb.

THE FEMININE PALACE

The womb space is like a palace where your feminine energy resides. I often refer to the womb space as "home." I believe we, as women, should see ourselves as royalty—as the beautiful princesses or queens we are—and our womb space is our palace, our home. When you place your attention on your womb space, it feels like you are coming home because you become peaceful, patient, strong, perceptive, and un-scattered.

Sometimes a woman will ask me, "If I don't have a womb anymore, do I still have access to this power?" The answer is Yes! The physical organ may not be there anymore, but the energetic space is still there. At the same time, however, it's important to know that when an organ is removed from the body, a vacuum is created in its place, and so we need to continue nurturing this center in order to keep it strong and vital. If you have had a hysterectomy, imagine the space where your physical womb used to be when you do the practices in this chapter. You are not at a disadvantage. I recently worked with a woman who had just had a hysterectomy and double mastectomy and had understandably felt traumatized by the process. After three sessions with me, she said, "I have never felt so feminine and beautiful in my life, and my husband and my sex life has not been this passionate since we first started dating!" One of our long-time students of *Art of Feminine Presence* is a transgendered woman. She chose to not have surgery on her anatomy, and instead swears by the power of embodying the feminine energy. Nothing sums it up better than when I first heard her say, "Ladies, it's not about the hardware, it's all about the software." Being feminine is about how you move and express your energy, not how you look on the outside or what parts of your body are no longer present.

THE DANTIEN

We each have a physical body, which consists of our bones, muscles, blood, etc., and an energetic body, which is the life force, or chi, that runs through and around our body. According to all healing, martial arts, and yogic traditions, one of the most important energetic centers of our body is suspended in the womb space (the lower abdomen for men). Most martial artists, Zen practitioners, and yogis call this energetic center the "Dantien." In Chinese Qigong, it is known as the "Lower Dantian," in Korean yoga, the "Dahn-jon," and in Japan, "Hara." This energetic power center is located in the center core of the body approximately three inches below the navel, inside the body. One of the Dantien's functions is to ground and receive yin energy from the earth. It acts as a storage place for heat and energy and is the center for physical strength and stamina. What is most fascinating is that this area has its own consciousness beyond the physical, and that consciousness leads us directly to our authentic power.

The Dantien is considered to be the "house" of physical communication, sensory awareness, and feelings. When something is going on in our environment or in another person, we have the ability to feel that in our own body. When I am listening to my surroundings not just from my logical brain but from my womb space, I can get accurate information from what I am feeling in my body. This is why we often say, "I have a gut feeling about this." These feelings from the Dantien are subtle, but the more you pay attention to your womb space the clearer the communication will become.[01]

Becoming more aware of your Dantien can have very practical applications in your life. If you listen to this intuitive communication while you are on a date, for example, you will save yourself a lot of time and possible pain. When you meet someone for the first time, don't just listen to your head's judgments about the person, listen to your womb space also. Your head may say, "he's

---

01 Johnson, Dr Jerry Alan, PhD, DTCM, DMQ (CHINA). Chinese Medical Qigong Therapy: A Comprehensive Clinical Text, (The International Institute of Medical Qigong 2000) p.91 and 92.

a great catch—go for it!" because his credentials look good on paper, but your womb space may pick up that he is not to be trusted in relationships or he's presenting a false persona. Listen to your womb space when you are considering working or spending time socially with someone. We don't always see what the body knows.

BREATHE FROM YOUR WOMB SPACE

When you place your attention and breath into your womb space, the mental chatter that says, "you can't do this," "you don't deserve that," "he won't be interested in you," "you are not good enough," etc., starts to quiet down. It's almost impossible to be self-conscious from that space, as you become peaceful, calm, and grounded. Often, an ecstatic feeling of joy is present. With traditional meditation, many people find it a huge challenge to still the mind and make the mistake of thinking, "if I tell the mind to be quiet, it will"—but that puts more attention on the mental chatter, and so it continues. However, if you instead bring your attention away from your mind and put it on your womb space, the energy will move away from the mental chatter and you will feel peaceful.

Before I walk into a room where I want to feel confident and have my magnetic presence "turned on," I first drop my attention to my womb space. I often put my hands on my lower belly to help focus my attention there, and it only takes me a few seconds before I feel the unmistakable state that comes from being centered in this place. If you only receive one thing from this book, my hope is that this would be it. I cannot stress enough how important resting in the center of your body is. Don't take my word for it, try it! Practice sending your energy and attention to the center of your womb space as often as you can, especially when you want to make a powerful *and* feminine impression. You will have people relating to you differently, immediately.

As you continue to connect to the inner core of your body, which goes up from your root chakra, through your womb space, and to the crown of your head, you will feel a stronger sense of your authentic self. Simultaneously, you will experience a sense of connection to your spiritual source and everything around you. You will feel enlivened and connected to a deep well of energy that you can draw from any time you choose. The center point of your womb space—your Dantien—is one of the easiest gateways to this vertical inner core.

Your practice: Take some time every day to place your attention and your breath on your womb space. One minute here, one minute there will do wonders. Feel the energetic power center that lies there and notice what it feels like. If you already meditate, I invite you to become even more aware of this area during your meditation sessions.

EXERCISE #5

(This exercise is included as a guided meditation on the Feminine Presence Meditations CD. **www.FeminineMeditations.com**)

Sit with your back straight—on the floor, on a cushion, or on a chair. Close your eyes, bow your head slightly, and bring all of your attention to the center point of your womb space. Imagine that at the center point of your pelvis is a small globe of light. Hold your attention on this globe for one minute. Now, imagine this globe is breathing. Imagine that the globe expands with every breath in, and the globe contracts back to its original size with every breath out. Take soft, subtle, easy breaths from this center point of your pelvis for a few minutes. Notice how you feel and what sensations you are aware of.

LISTEN FROM YOUR WOMB SPACE

The nature of a woman's body demands that in order to survive and thrive she needs to be in touch with her body. I once heard a female police officer give a presentation on how to prevent being attacked. She said that the number one thing that will keep you safe is not your ability to physically restrain someone but to "know your surroundings"—know where you parked your car, know if anyone is walking behind you, and, if you can't see anything, to feel your instincts and not doubt them. The instincts she was talking about come from inside the body. If you are not "in" your body, you miss out on this information and could get yourself into a potentially precarious situation. It is not your physical strength that will prevent an attack on a deserted street; rather, it is your heightened sense of awareness of your whole environment that will help you. That heightened sense comes when you are in your body, and most specifically when you are centered in your womb space.

Your practice: Imagine you have a set of ears attached to your womb space. Start "listening" to people and places from there. When you walk into a room of people, listen to what is going on from your womb space. What does it tell you about the energy in the room? Notice that all people send vibes, some positive and harmonious, others negative and dissonant. Your womb space naturally picks up on these signals from people.

Dr. Christiane Northrup, who has dedicated her life to women's health and personal development, says, "Women have the capacity to know what they know, with their bodies and with their brains at the same time, in part because their brains are set up in such a way that the information in both hemispheres and in the body is highly available to them when they communicate."[02]

I experience the proof of this often. A few years ago, I interviewed a woman for a position with the company I was working for, and, as I spoke with her on the phone for the first time, the core of my torso, from my throat to stomach, started to tense up. I gathered from my intuition that she was not an emotionally balanced person, even though everyone else in the company wanted her. Unfortunately, a year after she was hired and became CEO, the company started to collapse as a result of her incompetence and greed.

Have you ever had a situation like the above? Have you ever felt sensations at your core and decided to ignore them? I have. If you listen to the wisdom of your womb, it will support you in not attracting or being attracted to those who do not have the capacity for emotional maturity or deep love. It will help

---

02 Northrup, Christiane, M.D. Women's Bodies, Women's Wisdom (Bantam 1994) p32.

you not to waste time with the people you don't want to be around, and to start to tune in your signal to those you do.

SPEAK FROM YOUR WOMB SPACE

Most people communicate from an imaginary space a few inches above and in front of their forehead. It reminds me of the dialogue bubbles in cartoons and comic strips: Our attention is in that bubble and not connected to our bodies at all. As we search for what we are going to say next, or worry how others are judging our words, we become "not present." By putting all of our attention on our thoughts instead of inside our body, it is as if we are just a talking head on a stick. Needless to say, this does not create much intimacy in communication.

When I am being that talking head on a stick, I speak quickly and with a higher pitch, and it feels like I am spurting words all over the place without any real desire to connect. I am not present. But when I speak from inside my body, particularly from my womb space, I feel connected to the person or group I am talking to. I feel more comfortable and confident with my words; I don't have to go searching for them like I do when I am nervous. When I drop my energy lower, I speak slower, deeper, and in a more authentic voice. I become very present in a matter of seconds, and the intimacy increases instantly, as well as my magnetic presence.

Being "home" in your body is a fundamental principle in your attractiveness as a woman. When you are connected to your womb space you are more present to the moment, and people are noticeably more drawn in to what you have to say. You are perceived as a more trustworthy and safe person because you are not energetically invading others' space—but are instead centered in your own "being."

It's important to express your feminine essence through your voice. When we are not "home," we usually talk using a higher pitch and with a thinner and softer tone than we do when we use our authentic, powerful, and feminine voice. Practice letting your voice relax, drop, and express itself. Whenever I engage with someone, my practice is first to check in with where my attention is. I ask myself, "Am I 'home' in my womb space or am I in my 'head bubble?'" Time and time again, when I ground my energy into my lower belly, I feel the resonance between the other person and me dramatically increase. If you practice doing this, you'll find that many times the person or persons you are with will drop deeper into their bodies without consciously being aware of it. They will feel energized, secure and peaceful, and will often attribute that feeling to being in your presence.

Your practice: Imagine you have a voice box attached to your womb space. Talk to people from there. When you have a one-on-one conversation or speak to a larger audience, put attention on your womb space. What do you notice that is different from when you are talking from the space around your head? Notice if people's reactions to you change. Do you feel more of an intimate connection with the person you are talking to?

Nurture and respect the palace of your feminine energy—it is on your side.

In *Art of Feminine Presence,* we always start women training their focus on their womb space over any other part of their body. It's not because this is the most important part of the body. My work is about full embodiment and receptivity. The heart, of course, and all energy centers are very important. We start there because her pelvis is most often the first place she disassociates from and loses presence if she has too much attention on her, is too stressed, or doesn't feel safe. Over the years of teaching I have heard on many occasions that I should be focusing more on the heart area than the pelvis. If I am to help a woman be seen, be heard, be respected and well-compensated as a feminine presence in this world, I disagree. Being fully embodied in the lower half of the torso builds a foundation that gives us a grounded sense of safety and sense of our individual sovereignty, as well as the ability to act. If a woman does not embody her pelvis, she will not always feel safe and home in herself. Hence, if she is mostly working on embodying her heart, she will find that when she feels safe she will experience her heart open and loving. When she doesn't feel safe her heart will close. Do you sometimes experience that one minute you feel undefended, receptive, and open, and other times closed (even though you are trying to *not* be closed)? To get off the rollercoaster of your heart opening, but then closing in defense, spending time reclaiming your womb space so you fully inhabit it is critical.

We'll soon get to more practices that embody your feminine essence, but before we move on there is an important qualification to make. Who we are at our highest level goes far beyond our gender and sexual essence. We are all on an evolutionary path of consciousness, regardless of gender, and some accelerate quicker along that path than others. In the next chapter, we'll explore whether the feminine essence has an impact on our spiritual development and how it's possible, through igniting your feminine essence, to be hot *and* spiritual.

CHAPTER SIX SUMMARY

The womb space holds the power of our creativity, our strength, and our stamina. It is the "house" of physical communication, sensory awareness, and feelings. We pick up a great deal of information about others and our surroundings when we connect to this place in our bodies. Remember to:

Breathe *Listen* *Speak*

from your womb space. Notice how your conversations and relationships deepen when you do this.

CHAPTER SEVEN

HOT AND SPIRITUAL

It is through life, not out of it,
that the feminine will find the divine.

~Liana Gailand

The true essence of who we are goes far beyond our gender or sexual essence. At our highest level, we are spiritual beings. At the same time, we live in a world of opposites so that we can experience all facets of life: We cannot experience light without darkness, or what cold feels like without the experience of hot. If everyone were the same, we would not be able to experience ourselves as unique individuals, which is part of the richness of being human. To live a fulfilled life, we must experience both sides of our nature, our unique self *and* our spiritual self, the self that is inter-connected with everything around us. Life is a continuous and mysterious dance between the realms of the relative and the absolute, and there is a deliciousness and expansion that comes when we play in this world of opposites.

In order to grow in consciousness and experience ourselves as infinitely capable and connected to everyone and everything, we must participate in spiritual practices that help us experience our non-seeking, infinite mind; the mind that does not need to do anything or grasp onto anything in order to be happy. This truth can't be side-stepped. However, as we evolve, we must not get caught in the trap of thinking we need to transcend our humanness. Those I see doing this end up in trouble. They think that not giving attention to their sexuality, or their need to express "negative" emotions will lead them to enlightenment. This mindset, however, creates a breeding ground for dysfunctional relationships, or at least not very fulfilling ones. A conscious *and* functional person evolves spiritually while including and embracing their human qualities. Their focus is not just on waking up spiritually, but growing up to be a well-adjusted human. Freedom and joy in everyday life come through embracing opposites (like the feminine/masculine poles) and through disciplined movement towards true connection with the other inhabitants of the planet. Throughout this book, stay aware of "holding the paradox"—that at our core we are pure spiritual beings and yet we have a human body, brain, and sexual essence that affects the way we relate to others and how we offer our gifts to the world.

DOES THE FEMININE ESSENCE IMPACT OUR SPIRITUAL GROWTH?

I don't believe that the way to enlightenment is to become a perfect balance of masculine and feminine essence. We would do a great disservice to a talented young musician if we encouraged him or her to spend less time on their music lessons and more with their math tutor so they could become a perfect balance of both. Rather, we know instead to nurture them by supporting their creativity because their music is the gift they have to bless the world. Telling a young woman that she must spend as much time developing her masculine essence as her feminine essence has the same result—we blow out the flame of her gift.

That said, however, if we have the desire to transform our consciousness, we cannot be addicted to sexual pleasures and be over-identified with our gender, as that promotes thinking we are separate from others. What a delicate dance this is—even to describe it.

For clarity's sake, I'd like to return to the discussion of the three levels of awareness that lead to wholeness. We all have access to yin qualities and yang qualities within us, and it is a positive thing to have an equal proportion of both. All the inspiring people in my life, those who have a spark, an aliveness about them, who are manifesting in healthy ways, are quite balanced with both yin and yang qualities. They spend time in stillness and introspection, listening to inner guidance, and can slow their rhythm down when they need to. At the same time, they are very comfortable with making things happen, leading, taking action, and quickening the pace when the moment calls for it. The more I am free to use either yin or yang, given what the moment is calling for, the more powerful (from both an inner and outer perspective) I become.

The caveat is this: We are in women's bodies. We are human. We are women. We all have both a feminine essence and a masculine essence within us, although through my work with thousands of women I am convinced that about 95% of us experience much more joy and pleasure and are more present in the moment when we are connected to our feminine essence. Therefore, while we want to develop both our yang power and our yin power, we also want to keep our feminine energy alive. Can we do this and still express both? I believe we can.

Working with our feminine and masculine essences is a gateway to experiencing our divinity. My path towards being able to honor and love both the feminine and the masculine in me has brought more compassion to my heart and less attachment to how others should be. A woman who only honors the feminine and does not make full peace with the masculine inside herself and with men in general slows down her process of spiritual growth. A man who only honors one aspect of yin or yang does the same. In my work I've witnessed that the women who have developed strong masculine qualities often have an easier time allowing their strong feminine to be present. They respect both aspects of the divine.

People often say that having an intimate relationship can be the best spiritual practice there is. This is so because an intimate relationship encourages us to love and accept the opposite *as* we unite with it, thus feeling as though we are one with that opposite. An intimate relationship will also bring up all our "unwanted baggage", to examine and heal—if we choose.

THE MASCULINE SEEKS FREEDOM AND EMPTINESS

Since I began my journey with the feminine essence, I have been inspired by the work of author and teacher, David Deida. Deida has offered much clarity and wisdom to the discussion of whether embodying our primary sexual essence is central to our spiritual growth and attracting a conscious intimate relationship. Deida teaches that a man who is in touch with his masculine essence wants to experience himself as pure consciousness and emptiness, whereas a woman who is in touch with her feminine essence wants to experience herself as love, Light, and fullness. Together, these states represent the two seemingly opposing aspects of the divine.

A masculine man's desire for emptiness can manifest in many different ways. He may "zone out" in front of the TV or retreat from the family drama and go into "his cave." He may do this in his office, by taking a hike, or by going on a vision quest. The desire for emptiness is why men love to fix things: When a man fixes something or completes a task that is needed, there is a satisfaction that comes with its completion that feels like a "positive emptiness"—the need is no longer there. In that moment of completion, he can rest—even if it's just for a moment—before the next thing that needs his attention arises. For this reason, there are different forms of spiritual practices that are suited for either the "masculine essence man" or the "feminine essence woman" as they yearn to experience themselves as different aspects of the divine.

Masculine spiritual practices involve emptying the mind and body and achieving states of nothingness. Sitting to meditate for hours on end without moving is a masculine-oriented practice. In this practice, a man can experience more expanded states of consciousness where nothing distracts him from his own state of awareness. A monastic life where life's pleasures are taken away (simple food, simple room, and no sexual intercourse) is a masculine-oriented practice that, in many cases, helps people reach higher states of consciousness. To a woman in her feminine essence, however, this may not sound like any fun at all. When a masculine man practices non-dual meditation, his practice is almost always on resting as awareness. A feminine woman, on the other hand, will have more of an inclination to practice resting as love and light during meditation.

THE FEMININE DESIRES FULLNESS AND LOVE

Walk into a single man's house and then a single woman's house and you'll quickly see the difference between emptiness and fullness. A man's house is usually not decorated but is rather set up to be functional. When a man sets up his home, he looks at his living room and says, "Here's where the sofa will go. Here's where the TV will sit." A woman, on the other hand, says, "What colors will work here? How can I brighten this place up? I want to make this warm and inviting for anyone who comes to visit." A man sets up a sofa, a TV, and a bookshelf. A woman sets up a sofa, a TV, and a bookshelf and then adds some throw rugs, colored cushions, fabric to dress the room, flowers, matching drink coasters and tissue box covers. This is one way you, as a feminine essence woman, can make your life a work of art.

A feminine essence woman wants to shed light onto the world and wants to be seen as Light. The makeup and fashion industry have made billions out of this deep desire, but being seen as Light has much less to do with the smoothness of a woman's skin and much more to do with her inner light. A woman shines as Light when she radiates love to those she comes in contact with. She shines as Light when she feels the fullness and juiciness of her body, her emotions, and her gratitude for life. She is not a dried up prune but a glowing ripe plum who wants to experience the fullness of life without any need to fix anything.

Sacred dance or other movement meditations are feminine modes of spiritual practice, as they bring us into our bodies to feel sensations, emotions, aliveness, and the fullness of the moment. Anything that supports you to feel how full of love you are and how full the moment is can be a feminine spiritual practice, such as the practice of being fully present in conversations, in love-making, or while playing with your children. A woman wanting to live as love, Light, and fullness must ask herself these three questions:

1. What rituals and practices fill me up and make me glow?
2. Can I feel myself as the embodiment of love, even when life gets messy?
3. In what ways can I bring the divine through my body and express that?

You don't need to transcend into emptiness, into no desire, or into the spirit realms in order to become enlightened and free from suffering. The feminine asks, "How much can I love and receive love and experience myself as pure, full, ecstatic love while I am in this human body and facing human trials?"

Women have road blocks to spiritual development that don't apply as much to men. Women, for example, generally have a greater fear of separation and isolation than men. Women can also have a harder time speaking their truth when there is a chance of losing a relationship. One way we expand our consciousness as women is to move past the need to identify just with our birth family and close friends, fitting in only with what they expect of us; when we do this, we open our hearts wider than just to our socioeconomic group and have the experience of compassion for all living beings. This process gives us more strength and courage when we want to speak our truth and act in support of our entire global family but face possible rejection from our "tribe." The feminine longs more than the masculine to commune and be in an intimate relationship. A woman on a spiritual path is faced with the challenge not only of feeling full of love and light when she is in a relationship but also when she is alone and in pain.

The limitations of the feminine must be faced in order for a woman to experience her full potential and her divine nature more consistently. Men, on the other hand, have a different set of challenges and limitations. Understanding this reinforces the view that the feminine spiritual path is somewhat different from that of the masculine.

EXERCISE #6

Not every personal or spiritual growth practice works for everyone. Which practices have taken you, as a woman, into deeper awareness of your infinitely capable self, and which ones bring you to the present moment more easily and quickly? Consider that the practices that ask you to transcend everything and experience a void-like state may not be best suited to you as a feminine essence woman.

Which feminine practice do you want to explore this week that will help you connect to your unlimited spiritual essence?

SEX AND SPIRIT

The key to become a fully expressed woman is to marry the two forces of sexuality and spirituality, to create a relationship between the two so that they work together for you, not against you. They *can* live happily ever after together. You *can* be hot *and* spiritual.

We women have metaphorically severed ourselves at the waist and created a split between our sexuality and our heart and spiritual awareness. This split starts for most in early childhood. Taboos against sexual feelings are passed down from sexually repressed adults, and sexual abuse, whether overt or subtly intrusive, leaves children defensive around the lower part of their body. This cultural repression is reinforced by many religions preaching that spirituality and sexuality represent the forces of good and evil, respectively. [03]

Most women live from the waist up. If they do venture below the waist, they disconnect from their heart in the process, which causes all sorts of problems. Women who live only from the waist down often make bad choices in intimate partners. They attract men they think are hot, but who can't show real love or

---

03 Blackstone, Judith. The Enlightenment Process: A Guide to Embodied Spiritual Awakening, (Paragon House 2008), p. 131.

commitment, or men who don't have the capacity to love them but think they are hot and good in bed. Women who live from the waist up experience little juiciness and passion and have a hard time manifesting what they want in the real world. They may attract people who have a deeper capacity for emotional maturity and love but who do not turn them on. We all have moments of living below the waist or above the waist, but true empowerment—and your magnetic presence—come alive when both "power centers" communicate with each other.

EXERCISE #7

(This exercise is included in the Feminine Presence Meditations CD www.FeminineMeditations.com)

Sit upright so your back is straight. Place all of your attention on the center point of your vagina. Feel the internal muscles and the energy you feel there. It doesn't matter if you can't feel much sensation there at first. Gently squeeze and release your vaginal muscles to activate the energy there, and keep your attention flowing to that point in your body. Now, imagine that your vagina is breathing clear and subtle breaths. Continue for two minutes.

Now, place all of your attention above your waist, on the center point of your heart space. Notice that the energy here has a different quality to it. Flow your attention to this point in your body. Imagine your heart breathing clear and subtle breaths. Continue for two minutes.

Next, place your attention on your vagina and your heart at the same time. Notice what it feels like to connect to both of these points simultaneously. Now, imagine your vagina and heart breathing clear and subtle breaths together. Both points expand and release together. Continue for two minutes.

Practice this meditation as often as you can to encourage these two points in your body to communicate with each other.

For every fully expressed woman, there comes a time when she must embrace her sexuality. This energy is key to her life force. If she doesn't feel comfortable feeling her life force, she'll always cower away from living her purpose. This is difficult for many women as the inner sex kitten, or harlot, is a shadow part in many of us that we may not have made peace with. When we embrace this shadow (an unconscious part of ourselves that we have repressed), we are able to claim an integrated, healthy expression of our sexuality. From this space, we don't need to repress our sexuality out of shame, and we don't need to flaunt it to get attention and feel loved. This is why exotic dancing and pole-dancing in the form of a weekly fitness class can be so healthy for women; it's a safe place for us to express our sex kitten and feel the lower half of our body. However, it's also important not to get stuck there: If you keep living from only beneath the waist, you will keep the separation of sex and spirit in place.

Joining a pole-dancing class isn't the only way to start to express your inner sex kitten; if this feels too uncomfortable, start your exploration with some sexy music in the privacy of your own home—practice inhabiting your lower body and moving your sexual energy through your body with dance. When this powerful force is contained for your own pleasure, it can open your heart and upper chakras.

Since the first edition of this book there has been a wave of women (and men) who have built brands that promote connecting back into your sexual energy. In my opinion, many have over-sexualized the issue. On their social media feeds they post provocative pictures of themselves in order to show how liberated they are, and hope to build a larger tribe of women who can flirt and orgasm like there's no tomorrow.

Inhabiting your sexuality means you are inside your pelvis attuning to this beautiful aspect of the feminine. It's not about splashing your sexual energy everywhere. It's one important aspect of women's empowerment and spiritual awakening, but it's only one of many aspects.

Sheila Kelley, actress, dancer, and creator of *S Factor*, one of the first pole-dancing fitness programs, is an example of a woman who lives connected to both halves of her body. When Sheila teaches women exotic strip moves, she is playful and emanates love and a desire for all women to feel empowered. Her energy feels very wholesome and not "splashy" at all. Tina Turner is another example of a woman who knows how to ooze sexiness and is at the same time very connected to her heart and spiritual practices. These types of women are out there and are much-needed role models—look for them!

Aware, healthy, masculine men are looking for women who are connected to both halves of their body. What the coveted conscious and sexy mate really wants is a sensual, sexy woman who can also surrender to a greater power with an open and loving heart.

EXERCISE #8

It can be very difficult to admit that we have a sexy and erotic side to us when we are unable to own and feel comfortable with our sexuality. One way to determine how comfortable you are with your sexuality is to find out how easy is it for you to say aloud, "I am sexy and erotic." First, try saying this statement to yourself. Then "up" the challenge by saying this to someone you feel safe with. Be aware of any laughing or gesture that diminishes the power of what you are sharing. If you say it and then "cover it up" with laughing, that's a sign that you are not comfortable admitting it. As you continue practicing the exercises in this book your sexual and erotic power will become easier and easier to own. Your ease in saying this statement aloud will be a good indicator of how far you've come.

On a spiritual level, it does not matter if we are male or female, masculine or feminine. However, as we evolve to a higher consciousness, we can use polarity as a portal. We see that sometimes when two people join forces, the sum of their power together is much greater than if they were alone. That's the power of duality in relationship. When someone in their feminine essence joins with someone in their masculine essence, they can create something that is much bigger than the both of them. When Consciousness and Light, emptiness and fullness, come together, it's like a big bang—energetically, spiritually, and sexually.

It's time to start looking at more specific ways you can activate your feminine essence, ways that will affect both your inner world of spiritual growth and your outer world of relationships.

CHAPTER SEVEN SUMMARY

At the highest level, we are spiritual beings. At the same time, we experience ourselves as unique individuals. Both our uniqueness and our spiritual connection to all need to be nurtured if we are to experience freedom and joy.

The masculine essence wants to experience itself as pure consciousness and emptiness, whereas a woman who is in touch with her feminine essence wants to experience herself as love, light, and fullness. These represent the two seemingly opposing aspects of the divine.

Practice bringing together the two forces of sexuality and spirituality within you.

Ways to do this include:

- Bring your loving attention to your heart and your sexual organs at the same time. Feel how they are connected.
- Notice where you put your attention. Where your attention goes, energy flows.
- Embrace your sexual shadow, i.e., your inner sex kitten.

CHAPTER EIGHT

STIMULATE YOUR LONGING TO BE SEEN

Most of the shadows of this life are caused by our standing in our own sunshine.

~Ralph Waldo Emerson

All good advertising plays right into what women most want. If you flip through a woman's magazine and check out the ads, in most of them you'll see the woman looking at the camera and the man staring at her. He is not looking away or looking at the camera, he is looking at her, as if she is the most beautiful thing he has ever seen. Advertising strategists understand the nature of the feminine essence, as do all good movie makers and songwriters. They know that underneath her nonchalant façade, the feminine woman wants loving attention. She longs to be seen.

Isn't it true that the compliments that stay with you for months, if not years, are the ones that were directed to you because someone saw you at a deeper level, not just for what you did or what you were wearing? One of the most memorable gifts I ever received was from my brother-in-law the day we first met. He told me in his own way that he saw how beautiful I was, not just on the outside but on the inside as well. Even though we had only just met, I knew he could see what was special in me. To see a woman's beauty—both inside and out—is one of the most profound gifts you can give her.

In my younger years, before a "girl's night out," I would often go to a friend's house to get dressed and made up. Preparing for the evening, a glass of wine in one hand and an eyelash curler in the other, was half the fun. Amongst the talk of which lipstick to wear and what eye shadow to use, I would try hard not to let anyone sense how much I wanted to be noticed, how much I wanted to be told that I was gorgeous. I would rush to finish my makeup before everyone else, hoping this would be a sign that I didn't care so much about my appearance. What I know now that I didn't know then is that wanting to be noticed isn't a shallow desire. A feminine essence woman needs to be seen and acknowledged for her radiance, her inner beauty, and her grace if she is to bloom into an open, beautiful flower.

What does a "conscious" version of a woman who wants to be seen look like? She isn't someone who desperately wants others to think she looks hot so that she can feel good about herself. Rather, she is a woman who draws on her own strength and intelligence *and* who is not afraid to share her "glow." She shares her glow naturally through her smile, her body, her beauty, and her words, and she understands that through being happy and at ease with herself she is making the world a brighter place.

Within each of us, there is both a "witness" and that which is being witnessed. The part of us that is the "witness" notices our thoughts, our feelings, the people and colors around us, and everything else. The other part of us—those thoughts, feelings, people, and colors—is that which is being witnessed. The masculine essence primarily associates with the witness and the feminine with that being witnessed. The masculine essence likes to put his attention on things. He fixes things. He wants to be appreciated for what he does. The feminine essence, on the other hand, wants to be understood and seen for who she is without needing to do anything. She represents the flow of everything—conversation, emotion, decoration, etc. The feminine essence wants healthy loving attention, and she wants it often. This is not a desire sprung from weakness but from an impulse to grow. Healthy attention is like food and water: If we don't get it, we don't grow, and when we stop growing, we die. It's that important. A woman who is seen by the people in her life stands outs by her vibrancy, her health, her skin, and her smile. She is well fed, and it shows.

HOW TO GET THE ATTENTION YOU NEED

Women's circles and even slumber parties can be wonderful vehicles to foster self-esteem and self-worth. That's because they are places where we share ourselves, our stories, and our dreams—and they are witnessed. We might do each other's hair and makeup and talk about important things in our lives while other women witness us. This is how we women (or girls) make time to be seen.

Much of the attention women expect from men doesn't come easily from them because they are not wired that way. Women, on the other hand, can give other women that attention freely and naturally. When a woman receives the attention she needs from other women, she becomes less needy and controlling with the men in her life.

In the *Art of Feminine Presence* trainings, I help women release the magnetic power of their feminine essence, I use many "witnessed practices." I invite the women in my workshops to practice being witnessed by another while being "in" their bodies as they move, breathe, or walk with their feminine essence. Through this act of being witnessed, the power of the practice, whatever it happens to be, is increased a hundredfold. Women will often practice at home alone what we learn in the workshops, with great results, but they are always fascinated at how much easier it is when someone is there to witness them.

If you are not in a women's circle, or if you don't have close female friends who appreciate you and see the magnitude of who you are, then you need to find them and make time to be with them. Don't fall into the trap of thinking you are too busy for "girl time." When you do get together with your trusted sisters, make a deliberate decision to share what you see in each other at the end of your meeting, and watch how each other lights up.

SHRINK TO FIT

Many women have the tendency to shrink in the presence of others. They hold a subconscious belief that they should not take up too much space or do anything that looks like they are trying to call attention to themselves. Their voice becomes thin or quiet. They apologize often. They are overly humble. Their shoulders slightly hunch over. I have suffered hurtful blows at the hands of people who didn't like it when I shone or succeeded, and you probably have too. These experiences stay with us and motivate us to hide our Light (at least partially) under a bushel—we relate being seen with being hurt or rejected, and so we "shrink to fit." Sound familiar?

Almost all the patterns we are trying to unwind in our life got wound up in relationship to other people. It was other people's reaction, judgment, or behavior that stuck with us and sent the message, "it's not safe to do that again." In order to unwind any pattern it's most powerful to do that in relationship to other people. What I mean by that is that it's easy to read a book about being confident and mastering your fear. It's easy to train your body to stand, walk, and talk as a confident person when you are alone practicing. It's a whole other thing to be confident when those who represent the people who judged you earlier in life are in the room looking at you. When we are finally witnessed by another while we stand in a new empowering pattern, it is more likely to stick. My TEDx talk, *How to Be Unshakeable When All Eyes Are On You,* gets to the heart of this issue. We want attention, but we are afraid of it because of what we experienced earlier in life.

In Australia, they call this shrink-to-fit phenomenon the "Tall Poppy Syndrome." If you grow taller than the other poppies, someone will soon come along and cut you down to size. Being Australian, I can absolutely verify this. It's a culture where being one of the crowd so you don't outshine anyone else is applauded. And if you happen to acquire fame or success, you'd better believe that you are "just one of the boys (or girls)," otherwise you'll have your head cut off—metaphorically, of course.

The problem with this line of thinking is that if you are trying to escape judgment you'll never win. If you are big, bright, and bold, you will be judged for that ("Who does she think she is?"); if you are quiet, shy and unassuming, you will be judged for that too ("Speak up woman! You need some confidence!"); and if you try to please everyone, you will also be judged for that ("She should stop being so worried about what others will think"). Judgment is going to come, no matter what you do or who you are, so you might as well be a bright, beautiful, successful, joy-filled woman and be judged for that rather than a diluted version of who you really are.

I used to brush up against people who would accuse me of being arrogant. I could never understand why people experienced me this way, because I always saw myself as one of the "nice girls." I hated being thought of as arrogant. I didn't want those around me to think I felt I was "better" than anyone else. I wanted to be perceived as being on the same level as everyone else. But what I grew to learn was that the more comfortable I was with my own Light switched on, with my own healthy sense of competence in my area of expertise, the more everyone else was also comfortable with it. Over the years, I've made peace with sometimes feeling superior, sometimes feeling inferior, and I don't hear, "who do you think you are?" anymore. What I finally understood is that doing extraordinary things in this world does not mean we are any better than anyone else, it just means we're that much closer to being who we truly are.

INCREASE YOUR PERSONAL PRESENCE

Some women walk into a room and are noticed by many. They have an air of confidence about them that is attractive. They have a magnetic quality that draws us to them. Other women walk into a room and are almost invisible. They may comment that "no one remembers I was even there." The first group of women has "personal presence" and is comfortable "being seen," and the second is not.

Personal presence is a quality that can be developed more than you may realize, and I believe it is totally worth the effort. Women with a strong personal presence tend to attract people quicker and easier than the rest. When they speak, they exhibit more credibility. If you don't have your Light turned up to its brightest setting, people can't find you as easily. Without personal presence, the type of man you want won't be able to find you, and your perfect clients or employer won't be able to find you either. Without personal presence, that ideal relationship you yearn to have with your present or future partner will never come to be.

How you are noticed before you even say a word has a great influence on another's impression of you—and how you are noticed can be cultivated. I'm eager to show you how to develop a physical and energetic presence that will allow you to walk into any room and attract the attention you want. I want you to have that "IT Factor" that is beautiful and powerful and magnetic so that you can give your gifts to the world—and yourself—more easily.

The five fundamental practices to increase your personal presence that I will now guide you through are:

1. Be present inside your physical body
2. Feel your energetic presence
3. Move your physical and energetic bodies together
4. Turn on your primary sexual essence
5. Enjoy yourself and your movement

1. BE PRESENT INSIDE YOUR PHYSICAL BODY

Be in your body. Inhabit your body. *Where your attention goes, energy flows.* Send your attention to your body and notice what's going on in there. Actors, dancers, and martial artists often have a lot of personal presence, as they have a strong sense of physicality. They inhabit their bodies. They have to in order to succeed in what they do. Unfortunately, however, most people don't know how their body is feeling unless there is pain to bring their attention to it. Being aware of and present in your body is a skill you must have if you want to be a magnetic woman.

There is a difference between putting your attention on a part of your body and being *inside* that part of your body – inhabiting that part. Feel the difference right now by choosing your hands or your feet as your experimental area. First put your attention on your hands or feet. Now, with your more refined attention be *inside* your hands or feet. Feel the subtle difference?

One of the easiest ways to be present to the eternal moment of now and to amplify your personal presence is to be inside your body and to inhabit your center point of gravity, your Dantien (or a little lower in womb space). We explored this point in your body earlier in Chapter Five. When I connect to this center point, I instantly feel present and strong. I start to feel physical and energetic sensations pulsing through me. There is an "aliveness" there that others pick up on. I see this in women I work with all the time. When they drop their attention from outside their head to their center point of gravity their personal presence increases. Their energy changes from scattered to concentrated because their attention—which was previously focused on tomorrow, or yesterday, or what someone else thinks of them—is now brought back to the present and contained within their body. And when their energy is contained, it's easier to see them—literally. When I ask women in our trainings, "what did you observe when she was in her womb space?" the answers I hear the most are; "I felt more connected to her and wanted to get to know her more," or "I didn't judge her as I was in the moment with her," or "I remember clearly what she said," or "she was very magnetic so I was drawn in."

Once you inhabit your body, you can start energizing your movement. This does not mean moving in a crazy big way: Move with energy and purpose, don't just walk and move haphazardly. Create a level of intensity in your body that makes you feel alive. Many think they have to have confidence before they can move with energy and purpose—not true! If you start to move in an energized way, you will start to feel confident.

EXERCISE #9

Take a moment now to put the book down, and place your attention on your Dantien (2½ to 3 inches below the navel, inside, in the approximate center of your body). Feel what it's like to have all of your attention inside your body. Inhabiting your pelvis by sensing your pelvis from the inside. Next, stand up, and imagine that you are speaking to a group of people about something you are passionate about. Move your body and gesture in an energized way. Make small movements, but with a lot of energy and purpose, and feel the intensity in your body, particularly in your hands and arms.

2. FEEL YOUR ENERGETIC PRESENCE

Our energetic presence is both the tingling, vibrating energy we feel inside our physical body and the energy that radiates out from our body as well. This energy is something we can't see, but we can certainly feel it. It's always there, and we can, at any time, choose to feel this energetic presence or not. The conscious decision to feel your energetic presence is the mechanism that flips the switch to you effortlessly shining your Light and your radiance; in order to flip this switch, you need to first be present to the energy inside your body.

Take a moment to bring attention to your hands right now. Feel your hands and the energy that is inside them and surrounds them. You don't need to put the book down, just feel the energy there. If it's difficult to feel anything, you can shake your hands or rub them together for a few seconds and then pull them apart slowly to feel the energy easier. Can you feel this energetic presence in your hands? Feel that the more present you become to your hands the easier it is to be present to the moment. Now, see if you can feel this energetic presence through the rest of your body, extending up your arms from your hands. As you read this book, bring your attention to your torso and feel the energetic presence there. Now feel it in your legs. It feels good, doesn't it?

In addition to the energy you can feel inside your body, you also have an energetic presence that takes up a wide space around you. I think of this energetic presence as a beautiful bright "light globe" that surrounds each of us, extending a little more than an arm's length away from our body. We could also call it our radiance because at times it can start to glow. This energetic presence is always there, but we need to flip our own light on before anyone else can see it. Remember, the action that flips that switch and in turn increases our personal presence is our ability to feel our own energetic presence, both inside and around our body. The next integration exercise will guide you in how to flip this switch so that others can see you in a whole new way.

EXERCISE #10

Stretch your arms out to the side, with your palms facing up. Feel your energetic presence as much as you can, first in your hands and arms, then through your torso and the rest of your body. Imagine your energetic presence extending out from your body, a little over an arm's length away, as if it were a big, bright "light globe." Once you have a sense of this inner and outer energetic presence, experiment with the following instructions.

1. *Stand or sit, enjoying the connection with your energetic presence both inside and outside your physical body. Imagine that the outer layer of your energetic presence is still expanded a little over an arm's length away. The globe of light around you feels big and spacious. Notice what that feels like for a minute or two.*
2. *I invite you now to contract your energetic presence as small as you can—almost as if it were not there. Imagine that the outer layer is now just 1 inch out from your skin. Bring your hands in so that they almost touch your body, as if they signified the outer layer of your energetic presence. Keep your energetic presence contracted. Notice what that feels like for a minute or two.*
3. *Expand your energetic presence once again as you imagine the outer layer of your energetic presence a little past an arm's length away. Your hands comfortably outstretch as far as they can go in all directions to signify this expansion. Take a minute to feel what that feels like.*
4. *Again, contract your energetic presence as if the outer layer were again just one inch out from your skin. Bring your hands in as if they signify the outer layer of your energetic presence. Feel what that feels like for a couple of minutes.*
5. *Finally, expand your energetic presence out past your arms so it feels big and spacious, but this time also keep your attention on the center point of your womb space, the center point of your energetic presence. Notice what this feels like and how this state differs from just expanding your big, bright, "light globe."*

In as many moments of the day as you can, be aware of your energetic presence and expand it to arm's length and a little beyond. Take up your space as you stay connected with the center point of your womb space. Feel your energetic presence as big and bright, but stay connected to your core.

3. MOVE YOUR PHYSICAL AND ENERGETIC BODIES TOGETHER

When we move our physical body together with our energetic body, our presence and joy increases. Some of us tend to move in a very physical way—we look and feel heavier and more grounded. Others tend to move in a more energetic way—we look and feel lighter and a bit "spacey." But when we stride with a balance of 50% physical and 50% energetic, something magical happens.

Take a moment now to move one of your hands through the air in a very physical way, without any focus on your energetic presence. Watch and feel the dense matter of your physical hand as it moves. Notice what that movement feels like for a minute. Now, move your hand through the air in an energetic way, without any focus on your physical hand. Watch and feel the lightness of the energy in your hand moving through the air. Notice what that movement feels like for a minute. Finally, look at your hand and see that it has both a physical quality and an energetic quality to it. Now, move both your physical hand and your energetic hand through the air, as if they were moving as one. Notice what it feels like when you move both together with a 50/50 balance.

When I ask the women I am working with to share what they became aware of in each of the above modes, the most common response I get is that the physical felt heavy, the energetic felt light, and when both the physical and energetic moved together they felt more present in the moment, more alive, and more joy. I like to take this practice one step further and ask some women to walk the length of the workshop room in the three different modes, physical, energetic, and 50/50 balance. The power of the 50/50 balance becomes clear for everyone to see. When a woman walks with both her physical and energetic bodies in sync, she "pops." All of a sudden, she has the "IT Factor" that most of us want.

EXERCISE #11

Walk the length of a room and back three times in these three different modes:

- *First, walk with only your physical body. Feel the denseness of your muscles, joints, and bones as you walk.*
- *Second, walk with only your energetic body. Feel the lightness of the energy inside your body as well as the energy surrounding your body.*
- *Third, walk with both your physical and energetic bodies moving together with a 50/50 balance.*

Notice particularly what changes for you when you walk with both physical and energetic bodies together. Which mode of walking is more habitual for you? This week, if you tend to walk in a more physical way, bring more attention to your energetic presence. Extend your bright, spacious, radiant "light globe" around you. Get lighter. If you tend to walk more energetically, then add more attention to your physical body this week. Keep checking in with whether you are inside your body or not.

4. TURN ON YOUR PRIMARY SEXUAL ESSENCE

A woman's personal presence grows when she connects with her feminine essence, as does a man's when he connects to his masculine essence. Often, women will puff out their shoulders and chest with masculine energy in order to gain respect from a room and be seen. However, this does not work. Do you remember the three Feminine Activation Points from Chapter Five? When I used them to guide my volunteer to turn on her feminine essence, one minute she was standing there with not much presence and the next she was glowing. When a woman disconnects from her feminine essence, she disconnects from her vibrancy and her radiance, and as a result she is noticed less.

Who comes to mind when you think of a man who has a huge amount of personal presence? The names I typically hear when I ask this question include

Tony Robbins, Sean Connery, Hugh Jackman, and George Clooney. These are all men with a lot of masculine energy. I have yet to have anyone answer this question with an effeminate man's name. Who comes to mind when you think of a woman with a huge amount of personal presence? The names I frequently hear when I ask this question include Princess Diana, Michelle Obama, Gwyneth Paltrow, and Beyoncé. These are all women who exude a lot of feminine energy.

5. ENJOY YOURSELF AND YOUR MOVEMENT

How much can you delight in yourself and your own presence? Next time you walk from your car into the bank or grocery store, you might walk as you usually do, or you could choose instead to walk enjoying every step and every movement of your body like you've never enjoyed it before. We always have that choice—to be present to the inherent pleasure in our bodies as we move, or not. You can practice enjoying your movement with simple acts, such as when you brush your hair out of your face with your hand or shift your weight from one side to the other. As you feel the pleasure as you move, your magnetic presence will increase. We can easily see and feel the greater level of magnetism in the woman who walks down the street with an extra swing in her hips and more of a bounce in her step; she is noticed more because she is enjoying the simple act of walking down that street. To enjoy your movement, you must be in your body, with your "light globe" turned on. In fact, often just the invitation of enjoying your movement will automatically get you "in" your body with your energetic presence alive.

EXERCISE #12

First, isolate one of your hands and move it through the air without any attention on enjoyment. Then, experiment by moving your hand while asking yourself, "How much can I enjoy moving my hand?"

Next, isolate your hips and move them around in small circles as you feel the pleasure of this movement. If you can, walk a few steps around the room you are in, swinging your hips, while asking yourself, "How much can I enjoy moving my hips?"

You can do this exercise with any movement. Next time you want to turn your magnetic presence on, ask yourself, "How can I enjoy my movement right now?"

Women want to be seen and noticed, and it's okay! When someone gives you attention, tell them how much you appreciate it—don't let the moment slip by. When someone notices you and gives you a sincere compliment, let it sink in—don't rush to give one back. Embrace your longing to be seen and noticed and look for people and groups that will witness you. This is the path to bountiful, healthy, loving attention.

CHAPTER EIGHT SUMMARY

Wanting to be noticed isn't a shallow desire. A woman with a feminine essence needs to be seen for her radiance, her inner beauty, and her grace if she is to bloom into an open, beautiful flower. You can tell a woman who is seen by the people in her life by her vibrancy, her health, her skin, and her smile.

Much of the attention you expect to come from men may not easily come from them. Make sure you schedule plenty of time with your women friends, and when you meet, make a deliberate decision to share what you see in each other.

Notice how you might "shrink to fit." Does your voice get quieter? Do you hide your Light? Do you not share your talents with others?

There are five main practices to developing your personal presence. They are:

1. Be present inside your physical body
2. Feel your energetic presence
3. Move your physical and energetic bodies together
4. Turn on your primary sexual essence
5. Enjoy your movement

CHAPTER NINE

INCREASE YOUR RADIANCE

Pretty is something you're born with.
But beautiful, that's an equal opportunity adjective.

~Author Unknown

When a woman experiences her own beauty and the joy of feeling comfortable in her own skin, she radiates Light. When a woman is connected with her own love for life and her own self-worth, Light radiates out through the pores of her skin. It's not just men who are attracted to "Light-filled women;" women are also drawn to those who radiate a beautiful Light from within. Your radiance has the power to attract strong friendships, great business opportunities, and the right attention at the right time.

If you want to increase your radiance, it's not just about strengthening your inner Light but also about highlighting your outer physical appearance so it expresses more of who you are; each is just as important as the other. In this chapter, I offer some easy processes that can immediately increase your Light and attractiveness. As a result, you will have others notice and respond to you in a more immediate and positive way.

Earlier, I asked you whether your Light is usually switched on or off: If it is off, I want to help you turn it on, and if it is on, let's turn it up!

HOW I CHANGED THE WAY I LOOK

Growing up, I always felt like I was somewhat of an ugly duckling. I was the eldest of four children, and all were blessed with cute smiles and bright blonde hair, except me. My genetic makeup inspired mousy brown hair, a big nose, and big ears. I still remember my best friend in 5th grade telling me I wasn't one of the pretty girls but that maybe if I put some weight on I'd look better. I remember eating more after that in an attempt to look better. It didn't work.

I had an average-to-slim body all through school. In fact, it wasn't until my first year at university that I started to notice I was gaining weight. I had become bored with my studies and felt many of my friends didn't understand me, and so I had started staying up late at night, munching on junk food, and stacking on an extra 30 pounds. This made me even more disappointed, convinced that I would never be one of the "pretty girls."

Some years later, after gaining a few more pounds, I visited a seminar that was led by a so-called "intuitive psychic." I was skeptical but willing to listen. He talked about the power we all have to change anything in our lives. "You can be as successful, as wealthy, as happy, as fulfilled in a relationship as you want—if you are willing to believe it and take action," he said. I understood the power of intention and shifting limiting beliefs in order to create what I wanted, but I remember thinking, *Yes, it's true I can change a lot, but I can't change the way I look. I mean, I can lose some pounds and adopt a more flattering hairstyle, but I can't change the structure of my face or essentially how pretty I am.* A few moments later, I noticed the seminar leader standing right in front of me, looking down at me with a serious but caring face. "You can change *anything* in your life—you can even change the way you look," he said to me. *Whoa!* I thought. *Was this the psychic part of his routine?* He went on to explain that most of your outer appearance is related to how you think, feel, and act from the inside, which is why "mousy girls" can blossom as they gain more confidence in themselves and why many pretty girls in high school end up losing their physical advantage.

Today, I look and feel very different in terms of my physical attractiveness. When I show people pictures of me in my early twenties, they don't believe it's the same person. What is even more amazing is that I spend less time on my hair and makeup than I did back then, and yet I get more compliments on my looks today than I ever did before. You will hopefully be reassured that there's much more in your control than you may have realized as far as increasing your radiance from the inside out.

I now clearly see the correlation between how strong, healthy, and happy I feel on the inside and how that is reflected by my outer appearance. I know my radiance has grown because I have placed a strong focus on following my passions and becoming a joy-filled person. It's not just me: the *Art of Feminine Presence* energetic practices make *every* woman more radiant. I've also learned along the way what clothes accentuate my body shape, what colors make me look my best, and how best to wear my hair. I am not what the media would call a "perfect beauty," but I do make it a priority to increase my own radiance and beauty, knowing how it affects not only me but also those around me in a positive way.

ARE YOU HIDING YOUR LIGHT?

Many women say they don't really care about being beautiful, or they are past that, but in most cases I don't believe that to be true. A dear friend of mine said for a long time that she didn't want to put time or effort into making herself look beautiful; that it was just not that important to her. However, the rest of her life was all about beauty and art. She supported others in creating their own works of art and beauty, she painted, and she decorated her home with beautiful things. In our women's circle, however, her real desires were given permission to arise, and she started to realize that in the past her beauty had attracted unwanted male attention and negative circumstances. Now she sees that she is in a different part of her life, with the maturity and capability to say "NO." She is ready now to get in touch with her love for beauty and radiance in all aspects of her life, including the way she looks.

Have you put aside the desire to express beauty and radiance because you've had negative experiences with it in the past? Do you have negative beliefs about what beauty means? It's understandable if you have, as we often see beauty being used for manipulation, not good. But beauty can be used for good, too. We can consciously radiate our Light through our smile, our body, our hair, the way we walk, the clothes we wear, and the words we speak, and we can do it all for the higher good.

While it's true that your radiance is about much more than the redness of your lips, the shimmer in your eye shadow, or the shade of your fake tan, it does still have to do with your looks. There's no escaping this. Let's explore some ways to begin to brighten your light, first on the outside and then from the inside.

OUTER RADIANCE

I don't know any woman with high self-esteem who doesn't take care of the way she looks. These women know that the magnetic attraction they have is far greater when they look and feel great.

Take care of how you look. Be well groomed. This doesn't mean you have to look 100% your best all the time or be a slave to the fashion industry. Instead, know what clothes, colors, hairstyles, and makeup amplify your unique feminine essence. Discover the small things that will make the biggest difference to your appearance on the days you don't feel like putting in much time. I have figured out the way my hair looks best on the third day after washing it, for example, and if I only have two minutes to put on makeup, I know that a little eyeliner and mascara will make the biggest difference because my eyes are one of my best features. I also know what colors look best on me and so I make sure my comfy hooded sweat tops are in those colors, as well as my dressier outfits.

You might notice as you practice recommendations in this book that you will start to care more about how you look. Not from a vain or image-focused place, but from a natural desire to take care of yourself more. This happens when you start to inhabit your body and express more of who you are. It always makes me smile when I see women show up for the final day of our *Art of Feminine Presence* intensive looking so beautiful. It's clear that they have gravitated towards outfits and hairstyles that make them feel and look more feminine and radiant. Not once do I say during the training that you should look more feminine. Expressing beauty in a conscious way naturally arises as part of the process.

ACCENTUATE YOUR PHYSICAL ASSETS

What do you like most about your face, your body, your physical appearance? If you have great legs, learn how to show them off in a tasteful way. If you have healthy, shiny hair, wear it down more often. If one of your assets is your succulent lips, always have some gloss in your purse, ready to be pulled out at a moment's notice. If you don't know what your physical assets are, ask a trusted friend. One of my assets is my waist-to-hip ratio. I have a tiny waist, which makes my hips and butt look voluptuous. I used to hate this because my butt always looked bigger than it is, but I have since learned to make friends with it because I know now that it makes me look feminine. Understanding this as an asset, you'll rarely see me now in a top that doesn't hug my waist. And my legs are short, so you will rarely see me wearing skirts above my knee, either. It's important to know your assets and let them shine!

One of the first things to do in discovering how to accentuate your assets is to look at your silhouette in the mirror. Are you a woman who carries her weight in her waist and chest, or lower, in her hips, thighs, and butt? If you tend to carry your weight in your waist and have a slimmer lower body, accentuate your lower body; for example, you might look great in pencil skirts, slimmer fitting jeans, and shorter skirts, if you like your legs. If you tend to carry your weight in your hips, thighs, and butt, accentuate your waist and upper body; for example, you might look great in A-line skirts, belts, bootleg jeans, or slimmer-fitting sweaters and shirts.

USE COLOR

Explore what colors look good on you. Wear colors that highlight your hair, eyes, and skin. If you think you already know what colors are good for you, it might be time to reassess whether those colors still represent who you are today. I used to always wear black, for example—not necessarily because it looked great on me, but because it was easy. Don't get stuck wearing black, grey, or blue all the time; try some brighter or softer colors that look good on you, those that represent who you are on the inside.

There are three easy ways to use colors that will highlight your beauty the most, and those are to choose colors that match your hair color, eye color, and skin color. If you choose to redecorate your living room with new accents, like cushions, throw rugs, candles, and prints for the wall, the first thing you do is look at what color is already there—the wall color, the furniture fabric, and the floor color. You want to choose colors and fabrics that match the larger components of the room. It's exactly the same when it comes to choosing colors and fabrics to accent you as a person: You want them to match what is already a part of you— that includes your hair, your eyes, and your skin.

On the next sunny day, go outside with a mirror and really look at the color of your hair. Notice both the main color and also the highlights in your hair. My hair is medium brown with auburn highlights, so I am on the lookout for medium brown pants, skirts, and tops with a shade similar to that of my hair. Do the same with your eye color. Look closely at the type of blue, green, or brown your eyes are. My eyes are blue, but on closer inspection they also have turquoise and teal color tones in them. Therefore, the blues that suit me are not royal blue, navy blue, or gray blue but more blue/green colors like light teal or muted turquoise.

Skin tone color is also important. When you wear the wrong colors for your skin tone, it can make you look washed out. One of the most tried and true ways to determine what colors highlight your skin is to first establish whether your skin tone has blue or yellow undertones. As a general rule, blue undertone skin is usually pale, with reddish cheeks, while yellow undertone skin often has a sallow or golden complexion. Also notice whether there is a translucent quality or a more ash tone to your skin. With my skin color, I look for clothes with a pinkish beige or dusty pink versus gold (or yellow) because of my pale skin and pink cheeks.

All these color guidelines are just that—guidelines. Don't take any of them on as rules that you must stick to. I break the "rules" whenever I feel like it. Have fun expressing yourself with your wardrobe. Mix and match your seasonal colors for your own enjoyment, but be aware that some of them will make you shine more immediately than others.

TIME FOR A CHANGE

People often mark their transitions in life by a change in appearance. Humans have been doing this in every culture for millennia. A change in appearance helps us make transitions in other areas of our lives as well, and it might be just the right time for such a makeover in your own life to signify a reconnection to your feminine essence. If you have a friend who has a good eye for color and fashion, ask her to take you shopping. Get some new clothes, new colors. If money is tight, shop at Goodwill or a consignment store. Some of the clothes I get the most compliments on are ones I have bought at second-hand stores. Be courageous and throw out those clothes and colors that do nothing for you; they have been hanging in your closet for too long. It's time for a radiant change!

EXERCISE #13

Determine what colors make you look the most radiant by looking at your hair, eye, and skin color in the daylight. If you need to, ask a friend who is good with color for advice. Look through your wardrobe and throw out some of the clothes that don't highlight your appearance. It's time to breathe some life and Light into your wardrobe!

WHAT YOU PUT IN, YOU GET OUT

What you put into your body dulls or brightens your Light. I recently had two dermatologists approach me to ask if I ate a vegan diet. I told them I did. They both said they could tell because of the brightness of my skin. Many Americans eat a very acidic diet, which promotes premature aging and early disease, but eating an alkaline diet will radically increase your radiance. An alkaline diet consists of a lot of green vegetables, healthy grains, nuts and seeds, and very little dairy or meat or refined sugar, if any. It's unfortunate that hard science is only now catching up with the farming lobbyists, but better late than never; we are now finally learning that too much animal protein and not enough vegetables is a major cause of heart disease and other health complications, not to mention premature aging of the skin. A fun and motivating book I often recommend is the New York Times best-seller, *Skinny Bitch: A no nonsense tough-love guide for the savvy girls who want to stop eating crap and start looking fabulous!* In this book, authors Rory Freedman and Kim Barnouin share the hard facts on what makes us radiate with Light and what makes us look and feel heavy.

To be healthy, our skin needs both good food and appropriate hydration. It's important to hydrate your skin—both inside and out. Use an organic moisturizer that is paraben free and drink lots of water every day. Keep a water bottle close by at all times, and just keep sipping.

EXERCISE #14

Choose one dietary change you will make from this day on, a change that will make a difference in how healthy and radiant you look. Write this change on a note card, and stick it on your fridge—right next to the handle—so you will remember.

INNER RADIANCE

It's not always true that you can judge a book by its cover, but it often astounds me how much information I can pick up about someone's inner life just by the way they look—before they ever open their mouths. When someone is truly happy, they look more beautiful. When someone is following their life's passions, they look more vibrant. Over time, this can create a major change in their physical form. What makes you happy? What people make you happy? What pastimes make you happy? Bring more of these in your life, and watch how this changes what you see in the mirror.

The more happiness and pleasure you feel and can contain within your body, the more radiance you will exude. Have you ever had someone say, "you're glowing!" after you made love that morning, or after spending a rejuvenating weekend away? Often, women are not comfortable feeling huge amounts of pleasure in their bodies, and so it gets dispersed quickly. Start to notice when you find it hard to contain great amounts of pleasure in your body. The next time you are dancing or making love, practice feeling the pleasure you generate by keeping it inside your body rather than dispersing it by making loud noises or large movements. This may sound counter-intuitive, but try it. See if you can feel the subtle difference I am describing. If you practice keeping your Light contained inside your body and your energy field, it will feed you, and, in turn, that Light will brighten and radiate out to all those you want to bless with it naturally. When your Light builds intensity within you, it can only radiate onto others.

Acknowledging where you are leaking energy is the flip side of containing your energy. Every relationship, every business deal, every life choice has both a cost and a benefit. If there are any people, situations, or choices that drain you more than fill you up, it's time to make some decisions about how you want to spend your time and energy. In order to increase your radiance from the inside out, you must be willing to cut off or plug up the holes that are causing you to lose energy.

EXERCISE #15

Don't be afraid to show how much pleasure you feel inside you this week. Smile more. Let your radiance shine through your face.

RADIANT GLOW

A metaphor that best describes how a woman radiates from the inside out is that of a light globe. There are three ways a light globe lights up a room, and those are through the filament, through the globe itself, and through the light that fills the room. A woman is no different.

The filament in a regular light globe is like the center point of your physical and energetic bodies. In Chapter Six, "Womb Wisdom", we called this point the "Dantien," or the center point of your womb space. The stronger the wattage of the filament, the brighter the globe and therefore the glow in the room will be. Your feminine radiance works the same way. It is not something you need to project out to try to make others notice you; rather, it comes from inside you. Your glow brightens as you strengthen the energy inside your body, particularly the energy in your womb space.

As you continue to read this book, bring your attention to the center point of your womb space. Imagine a ball of light suspended about 3 inches below your navel and inside your body. Now imagine that this point of light is like the filament of a "light globe"—the stronger it gets, the more radiant your glow becomes. To build the energy at this point, direct more of your attention to this space. Remember, where your attention goes, energy flows. As you naturally breathe in, your stomach will expand and fill with air, and as you breathe out, it will relax. As you breathe out, slightly contract your stomach muscles and buttock muscles, bringing even more awareness to this point. When you flow your attention to your womb space, your radiant glow increases. I have seen this happen with every woman I have worked with, with no exceptions.

The second way a "light globe" lights up the room is through the "light globe" itself. The globe represents your energetic presence that is inside your body and extends out a little past an arm's length. Feel your energetic presence right now; it's the energy that runs through your body that feels light, tingling, and joyful. It might be easier to feel it in your hands first and then in the rest of your body. Now, imagine this energy extending out from you and creating a big, beautiful light that surrounds your body. This is your "light globe." Imagine that this globe is getting brighter and brighter. Remember, you are not trying to project your radiance to light up the room; you want to keep all your energy and Light contained within this "light globe." It should feel expansive and inherently joyful. When a woman has her attention on her womb space and at the same time fills her "light globe" by feeling her energetic presence, her radiance increases tenfold and immediately.

The third aspect of the "light globe" metaphor is the light that fills the room. Think of the light in your bedroom. The bulb does not need to project itself into the room to light it up; rather, it's the filament and the globe that light the room. It's the same with your radiance. Stay home in your womb space, feel your energetic presence expanding around you, and you will have already filled the room with your Light. No effort is required.

Increase your radiance and allow your body and your life to be a work of art to positively affect others. Your form of art could be anything—from wearing beautiful clothes to doing your makeup, wearing colored scarves, walking, dancing, playing music, or making love in an artful way. Decide what your unique form of beauty is, and express it. I have become acutely aware of the timeless importance of beautiful radiance: Its power and the way we relate to it are much more than skin deep.

Your feminine radiance is magnetic, so be conscious of the attention you try to attract. After all, the attention you're really seeking isn't from fleeting sexual encounters with a commitment-phobic male, or attention inspired only by your neckline, leaving nothing else a mystery, is it? No, the attention you—and all women—truly seek is the attention that will help you share more of your unique gifts with the world. Honoring your feminine radiance and the work of art you truly are is the surest way to get you there.

CHAPTER NINE SUMMARY

Your radiance is about much more than the redness of your lips, the shimmer in your eye shadow, or the shade of your fake tan. Nevertheless, it does have something to do with what you look like—there's no escaping this.

TO INCREASE YOUR OUTER RADIANCE, YOU CAN:

- Accentuate your physical assets. Know what parts of your body are most attractive, and wear clothes that bring attention to these parts.
- Wear colors that highlight your hair, eyes, and skin tone, as well as your personality.
- Eat an alkaline diet full of fresh fruit and vegetables. Drink lots of water.

TO INCREASE YOUR INNER RADIANCE, YOU CAN:

- Feel more pleasure and happiness in your body and contain it so it feeds you.
- Flow attention to the center point of your womb and heart space.
- Feel your energetic presence extend out from your body as if there were a beautiful big, bright light around you. Don't try to project your radiance.

CHAPTER TEN

WARMTH AND MYSTERY

Without mysteries, life would be very dull indeed. What would be left to strive for, if everything were known?

~Charles de Lint

There are two energies of a feminine essence woman that both men and women are especially attracted to: Her warmth and her mystery. Warmth is what leads a man to ask a woman out again on a second date, and mystery is what keeps him interested. Warmth is what makes other women feel comfortable and open with her, and mystery is what keeps them engaged. These energies may seem at first to be opposites, but as we'll explore in this chapter, when both are expressed in your own unique way, your magnetic presence comes alive. As you read about these two charismatic states, notice if you tend to express one more than the other, and stay curious about ways you could enhance both.

WARM IT UP

Who comes to mind when you think of a "warm" person? It might be a celebrity or someone you know personally. What do they feel like? What do they look like? They probably feel very welcoming, friendly, and open-hearted. When I picture a woman who expresses a lot of warmth, I see her smiling a lot and being affectionate. She's comfortable with starting conversations, especially about the other person. She's not afraid of direct eye contact, but it's soft and light. She has an open body posture; her arms are dropped to her side so she's not guarding her heart.

When you share your warmth, people want to be around you more. Your warmth makes them feel comfortable and welcomed, not intimidated. If you are already a confident, articulate person, or if you are in a leadership position where others look up to you, expressing more warmth is highly important. If you tend to have others feel intimidated or diminished by your presence, it might be because you don't express much warmth.

The time to "warm it up" is when you first meet people. Whether it's on a first date or a first meeting with a new client, be genuinely warm, and show that warmth through your eyes, smile, voice, and body posture. Your warmth gives potential partners or potential bosses and colleagues the sense that you are easy to be around—a huge factor in getting a call back. Don't be gushy or give everything away about yourself in the first few minutes, and don't over-accommodate to please. There is a difference between being warm and inviting, and not losing yourself trying to impress others.

If you are a presenter or a speaker of some kind, make sure you sprinkle your unique version of warmth throughout your presentation. Before people buy from you or follow through on what you say, they need to know, like, and trust you. If you shoot videos to share your message, start by "warming it up," at least in the first thirty seconds. Warmth is a great doorway to your audience feeling that you are a likeable, trustable person.

DON'T GIVE IT ALL AWAY

Who comes to mind when you think of a "mysterious" person? Again, it might be a celebrity or someone you know personally. What do they feel like? What do they look like? I picture someone who sits back and doesn't share much at first. Even though they may keep to themselves more than others, there is a spark about them that is attractive and draws people in to want to know more about them. They emit an energy that makes them seem interesting. When I think of celebrities that emanate mystery, I see them in photographs where they are not smiling but instead have an expression that says, *I have a secret—do you want to know what that secret is?* They may look at the camera, but they do so out of the corner of their eye or over their shoulder. Victoria's Secret has made millions from playing on this attractive quality of mystery. In most of their photographs, the models are not smiling, and they do not look warm, but the energy of mystery is palpable. Women who express a lot of mystery are intriguing; they make you feel like you want to get to know who they are at a deeper level. Great respect often comes with this mystery, as it's a mature woman type of energy.

Sometimes women see other women being mysterious and call it manipulative or putting on a façade to capture a man's attention. When I talk about "mystery," I am not describing being closed off to others or being fake or manipulative. The mysterious energy I am talking about can be playful, and it is a game that can be played to increase attraction and sexual polarity between the masculine and the feminine. We can choose to play this game either consciously or unconsciously. When we choose to play it consciously, it is fun and healthy for all players. Mystery allows the man to "open the gift" of a woman, as opposed to her showing it to him right away. A man wants to be in the presence of an open and warm woman, but he loves even more to "open" her himself. He likes the chase.

EXERCISE #16

Which one of these seemingly opposing energies— warmth or mystery—do you express more easily—often unconsciously? When I ask every woman in the current training group I'm with, at least one-quarter of them get it wrong. They think they lead with one of these choices, but everyone else in the room giggles because they lead with the other. If you're not sure, ask a couple of trusted friends for some honest feedback. Then ask yourself, "How can I express the opposite state more in my interactions?"

Here are some suggestions:

Express More Warmth

Ask yourself, "In what ways can I move my body and use my eyes and voice to express more warmth?" For example, you could smile more, use appropriate touch, or open your body posture so you are not covering your heart area when you talk. Or you might smile through your voice to make it more friendly and welcoming, soften your eyes, or not be afraid to share personal stories.

Ignite More Mystery

Ask yourself, "In what ways can I move my body and use my eyes and voice to express more mystery?" For example, you might look at someone out of the corner of your eye, try silence, or slow down your walk. Or you might lower your voice. Or perhaps you could try not being afraid to listen more with an inquisitive ear and not share every possible detail about yourself. When you create asymmetry in the body, this creates more mystery. Turn your shoulders or hips sideways from the person you are speaking to, which naturally creates curves in your body. This way, you will not be directly facing the person when you talk to them. Many women naturally do this when they are flirting with someone they are attracted to or dancing in a sensual way.

LIGHT-HEARTED SERIOUSNESS

When the energies of warmth and mystery come together, a woman can embody a powerful state that I like to call "lighthearted seriousness." Many women guard against being too feminine in fear that it is weak and that they will be perceived as "ditzy" or "flighty." This is an understandable fear because many women who don't own their feminine power come across this way. But when a woman has a seriousness about her, she is anything but "flighty." She has a clear mind and clear boundaries and doesn't always just laugh things off. People listen to her when she starts to speak. People want to hear her opinion and stories. Women and men alike perceive that she is not a push-over and that she will fight for what is "right" if she needs to. They perceive this from the way she walks, the way she talks, and the way she uses her energy.

It's interesting to note, however, that many women do not come across as having this kind of power. Instead, their fears are realized and they are perceived as "weak" or "flighty" because they are too busy trying to please everyone else by being overly nice. Yes, it's great to be a nice person, but these are not the women who end up gaining the most respect from others in the room.

The seriousness that I describe must come with a light heart. It's not heavy or boring, but it is a force to be reckoned with. Women who find it easy to be serious and are seen that way need to check to see if this seriousness is partnered with a light heart. The world is not going to end if you let go and "lighten up." If you do not bring your warmth into the picture, the seriousness may very likely be perceived as righteous, controlling, or masculine.

Be aware of the level of "light-hearted seriousness" you bring to your interactions. People will trust and respect you more if they feel you have a bit of an "edge" to you, in contrast to you always being sweet, soft, and nice.

EXERCISE #17

What are some ways you deflect your seriousness in interacting with others? For example, do you giggle a lot in conversation to lighten the mood, use a higher or softer voice than your authentic tone, or avert conflict with a funny comment?

Practice adding more seriousness to your interactions, especially when you want to gain the respect of the room.

Now you know how to turn your Light on with this beautiful balance of warmth and mystery, it's time to look at what might get in the way of all of this. There are certain obstacles that women face more than men on their path to being seen and heard in a powerful way. These obstacles need to be addressed *before* you hit stressful times or high-stakes moments, because it's sometimes hard to see them, even when they are staring you right in the face.

CHAPTER TEN SUMMARY

There are two seemingly opposing energies that both men and women are especially attracted to in women—warmth and mystery. Be aware of which energy you feel more comfortable expressing, and practice the one you don't embody as much.

Warmth feels inviting and welcoming and can be cultivated by smiling more, using a friendlier tone in your voice, and standing with an open body posture.

Mystery feels fascinating and enigmatic and can be cultivated by being quiet, using a softer lilting tone in your voice, and standing with an asymmetrical posture.

Be aware of the level of "light-hearted seriousness" you bring to your interactions. People trust and respect you more if they feel you have a bit of an "edge" to you and are not always sweet and nice.

If you have not already downloaded the free guidebook that goes with this book you can do that at: **FeminineGuidebook.com** and record your realizations there.

CHAPTER ELEVEN

HER BLIND SPOT

Feeling and following what we want requires that we distinguish between our "hidden conditioned wants" and our "conscious heart-felt wants."

~Tej Steiner

We all have a "blind spot" that blocks us from seeing and feeling what we want. Many of us drive down the road of life in the direction we think we should be going, and yet we have no idea that our true desires are completely hidden from view. We talk ourselves into thinking we want one thing, and yet the longing in our heart is for something else. In order to create the life you want, you must be able to notice when what you desire starts to move out of your direct view and into your blind spot. After all, if you cannot feel and acknowledge what you desire, you will not manifest it in reality. In this chapter, we will explore why women often don't let themselves feel their deepest desires, and how you can more easily discern the difference between what you think you *should* want and what would *really* make you feel fulfilled.

Earlier in my career, while working for a personal growth organization, I suggested my team meet with a trained facilitator, believing that each staff member needed help getting clear on what they wanted to achieve the coming year. Everyone except for me, of course. And, of course, the quirk of fate was that much of the attention fell on me during the course of the day, and I was the only one shaken from the experience.

We were all asked the same question: "What do you really want to be doing in this next year of your life, particularly in relation to this organization?" I felt very clear about my answer and was strong from the get-go. "I want to continue as director of my department and bring in more teachers and facilitators to help us offer the best programs we can," I shared. "I enjoy being the connecting point for the best teachers in the country to come to work with us. I want to learn as much as I can from them." After what I felt was a confident and impassioned presentation, I was shocked to see ten blank faces staring at me. The facilitator of the circle asked, "Who feels that this is really what Rachael Jayne wants?" To my shock and fascination, everyone in the room shook their heads. I listened with one eyebrow raised as one colleague asked with amusement, "Don't you want to be the one teaching from the front of the room now?" Another added, "I don't get that you want to keep helping other teachers get their message out; you want to get your own out—you are ready." As I listened to this, there was a part of me that was scared and confused, but another part was screaming YES! I was amazed that everyone in the room had seen the same desires trying to break free from my heart—everyone except me. I had not been aware of my own transparency, and therein lay my blind spot.

The function of our blind spot is not to make things harder for us, even though sometimes it may seem like that. Rather, the blind spot's job is to keep us safe—safe from harm, safe from pain, safe from persecution, safe from rejection, safe from loneliness. In order for me to feel safe and accepted as a member of the group I was in, I hadn't noticed what it was I had really wanted until it was reflected back to me. For me, and for most of us, there are many ways, both great and small, where we deny what we want so that we can remain "with the crowd." Although this protects us from perceived harm, it does not serve us in our goal of reaching our potential.

WOMEN FEAR SEPARATION

I believe the feminine's greatest strength is her desire and natural ability to create connections, build strong relationships, and care for those around her. We women do this every day, whether at PTA meetings, in our business networks, in our homes, or within our circle of friends. Ironically, this strength can also work against us, and our fear of separation can become the reason we cut ourselves off from feeling many of our own heartfelt wants.

I can still feel the extreme discomfort of my internal cringe whenever I am singled out for excelling at something. I feel anxious if I am put on a pedestal in the company of a group of peers that is attempting to do the same things that I am doing. Even though a part of me is ok with accepting praise and thanks, another part of me feels this "singling out" is somehow unsafe. What about you? Is it possible that you are out of touch with some of your desires because of a fear of success or failure, or that it will somehow lead to a disconnection from your family or peer group? I find that even in my most loyal and dear relationships my voice at times becomes weak, and I have a hard time saying what I want because I don't want to be rejected or put a rift in the relationship. Are you out of touch with some of your desires because you may have to say uncomfortable things and make changes in your life? In what ways are you squashing your voice or hiding what you really feel? What are you afraid of losing if you *really* go for what you want?

It's difficult to be aware of your blind spot without the help of others to point it out to you. They can see what's there when you can't. When you bring to mind what you *think* you want, question it. Don't take it for granted that it's really what you long for. Watch out for rationalizations and ask trusted friends or mentors for their sense about what you share. Remember, your blind spot is trying to keep you safe from something that it perceives to be a threat. If you ever hear yourself saying, "I don't really want a relationship right now, I am too busy," ask yourself, "Is this true, or am I just scared of more disappointment?" If you ever hear yourself saying, "Yeah sure, I'd love for you to work with me on this," ask yourself, "Is this true, or am I just afraid of how they'll feel about me if I say no, I'd prefer to do it myself?" Keep feeling into your deepest longings, even when the fear and reality of possible separation is present.

HOW DO YOU KNOW WHAT IT IS YOU REALLY WANT?

How do you know if you are doing something because it is truly what you want or if you are doing it because it's what's expected of you? Is the reason women aren't reaching top executive positions at the same rate as men because of an impenetrable glass ceiling, or because they don't have the same desire as men to be in that sort of work environment? Is the real reason more women than men are continuing to take on the role as primary caregiver and homemaker because they have been culturally forced to do so or because they have a stronger *desire* to do so? We women have different brains and bodies than men, and we're on a slightly different evolutionary path than men in some ways, so these questions are not easily answered. Even if women earned the same money and claimed as many top executive positions as men, that would still not assume that women have reached true equality with men; all that would conclude is that we have successfully been able to squeeze the round peg of a woman's desires into the square hole of the masculine world.

HABITS VS. HEART'S DESIRES

It's critical to listen to your heartfelt longings. This is a particularly challenging task for women because we often run on automatic pilot, taking care of everyone else's desires before we pause and feel our own. Knowing the difference between your habitual response and what you really want is important because:

- You create what you want faster when both your heart and head are working together instead of pulling you in different directions.
- You can create more of a fulfilling life for yourself.
- You can be a better support to others in following their passion rather than their expectations and attachments.
- When you learn to connect to your own heart, you connect with others

more deeply, in turn bringing more compassion and peace to a planet that desperately needs it!

- When you are connected and "tuned in" to your heart, you are more likely to create what is best for all concerned.

There are five primary keys that will help you discern the difference between your heart's desires and what you think you "*should*" be, do, or have.

Key #1: *Pause Before You Habitually Respond*

When someone asks me a question, I sometimes respond very quickly with my answer before "checking in" with how I feel and what I want. For example, a friend may suggest something for us to do together that evening and ask, "Is that ok with you?" and I will answer, "Sure," before I've even thought about it. To first be present with what you are feeling—physically, emotionally, and energetically—takes at least 10-20 seconds, and then to ponder what you want, given how you are feeling, takes more time. A quick response may be a clear sign that you are reacting from conditioning. Whenever I ask a client how they feel and they answer me without a pause, I can be almost certain that they are answering from their head. The information on how you feel comes through your body, particularly your heart chakra, not your head.

To practice key #1, I invite you to pause before you answer questions like "How are you?" or "Is this ok with you?" or "What do you want to do now?" Think of it as a 10- to 20-second delay before responding. If you need more time, take it. First feel into how you're feeling and then what you are really wanting. When making a decision about what to eat, what to wear, or what to do on a Saturday night, take the time to "check in" before you respond. A client of mine now hangs up the phone after a friend or family member asks her if she can do something; after their request or question, she says to them, "I'd like some time to consider this, and I'll call you right back." It may seem a little strange when checking in on minor details, but most of us go about our day a slave to our habitual patterns, and that needs to stop. This ongoing practice will help you get in touch with your heart's desires when it comes time for the larger decisions to be made.

Key #2: *Feel Your Authentic Feelings*

The practice of feeling what lies underneath the surface of your persona is essential in the process of discerning what it is you truly want. This takes awareness and commitment. We all have behaviors that guard us from feeling our feelings at times. These keep us safe from the pain and loneliness we have buried inside ourselves. Most of us use at least one of the following to protect ourselves from feeling our feelings: Food; alcohol; TV; sex; excessive time on the computer; shopping; over-working; or always staying busy. Do any of these ring true for you? Sometimes it's easy to see our patterns, and sometimes it's more subtle.

One of the ways I notice that I am cutting myself off from feeling my feelings is when I'm being critical of others. Over ten years ago, my husband and I moved to a new city in a new state where we didn't know anybody. Not too long after we arrived, I noticed how critical I was being of some of the new people I met. The wise part of me knew that my being overly judgmental and critical was a defense, my not wanting to feel my underlying feelings of loneliness and fear, and so I started to make myself more aware of this. One night, instead of continuing my judgmental dialogue, I walked upstairs to my bedroom and just sat quietly, with the intention of feeling my feelings. I sat there for a minute or so, feeling the sensations and energy in my body, when I was met with a feeling of sadness and loneliness. It washed over me, and tears came. Instead of trying to work out what the feelings were about, I sat there, feeling them. I didn't wallow in them or judge them, I let them be. Within what seemed to be about 10 minutes of sitting with these uncomfortable sensations, I felt the emotions subside, as if a wave had just moved through me and out of me. I felt peace. I then asked my heart, "Given that I am feeling sad and lonely, what do I want?" The answer was clear: I wanted to have fun, supportive, and spiritually-aware friends who were here in my new city. I missed my friends I had left behind, and I wanted to re-create great friendships in this new place. Now that I was willing to *feel* how much I wanted like-minded people in my life, I could start to put more attention on being open to attract them—which I did in spades.

No emotion is inherently "better" than another. Some certainly feel better than others, but if we judge the "lower" emotions as not good, we try to cut ourselves off from feeling them and the information they are trying to send us. Be aware of how much you judge the more challenging emotions of sadness, fear, anger, depression, etc. When you feel emotionally "down," don't beat yourself up. It's great to be a positive person, but putting aside your authentic feelings all the time in order to feel some false sense of happiness and success does not work in the long run. You might be fooling yourself, but probably no one else.

Your invitation with key #2 is to limit the behavior that most guards you from feeling your feelings. When this behavior or defense wants to take over, stop! Without opening the fridge, pouring the usual evening's glass of wine, spending more time on the computer, or blaming others, just sit and ask your heart, "How am I feeling?" and "Given how I am feeling, what do I want?"

Key #3: Follow the Joy

In the moment you connect to something you *really* want, you feel more joy than you had seconds before. You don't need to manifest it, you just need to feel the desire and possibility of it. Granted, fear may arise pretty quickly after that because part of you gets scared that you may not be able to achieve it, but joy always comes first.

During the day, you might find yourself at different levels of joy, depending on what is going on. You may have just heard some bad news, or you may be physically unwell, and your joy will go down. Or, you may have just heard some great news, or you may be feeling more vibrant than usual, and your joy will go up. One of the many reasons I love the teachings of Esther and Jerry Hicks, authors of *Ask and It Is Given* and the books in the Abraham-Hicks series, is because of their clear description of what they call the "Emotional Guidance Scale," similar to what I call your "Joy Meter." On the lower end of the "Joy Meter" are not-so-joyful emotions such as grief, sadness, anger, and discouragement (low joy); on the top end are more joyful emotions such as peace, love, excitement, and happiness. We become more conscious creators of our life when we can consistently move up this "Joy Meter" intentionally so that we feel more happiness in our life and therefore attract more of it in.

When you put your attention on the feeling of having or doing something you think you *should* want, your joy level does not go up. You may think it's a great idea, or one that could make your life easier, but you will not feel a surge of joy in that moment. But in the moment you connect to the feeling of having or doing something your heart really wants, your joy will automatically go up.

Your invitation to practice key #3 is to become more aware of what feels joyful to you. Notice where you are on the "Joy Meter" when you bring to mind the things you *think* you want. When you become aware of yourself getting excited or inspired, follow that joy!

A mentor of mine and master teacher of this practice is Tej Steiner, the creator of Heart Circles. A Heart Circle is a group of conscious people who come together with the intention to discover what it is they *really* want. The two central questions used in a Heart Circle are:

1. How am I feeling?
2. Given how I am feeling, what do I *really* want that will move me up the emotional scale to a more joyful state?

These two questions provide a beautiful balance in acknowledging your authentic feelings and using them to clarify what it is you want that will raise your joy. I have been in various Heart Circles for many years and find it to be an extraordinary support for me in discerning the difference between what I think I *should* want and those real desires that are hiding in my blind spot. Steiner says, "to sustain joy requires that we focus on what brings us joy; on what we truly want in any given moment, on what feels 'right' to us, and on that which we are passionate about feeling, doing, or having."

Key #4: *Expand Your Thinking*

You can't feel your deepest longings until you start believing in your greatest potential. Unfortunately, many people don't believe they have a choice to live a life that is any better than the one they are living. When you don't have access to your basic survival needs, it's nearly impossible to dream big. If a woman has only ever been in abusive relationships, it's difficult for her to believe that a relationship could offer her freedom and unconditional love. Likewise, how could a woman from her corporate cubicle know that she might love working for herself if she has only ever been told that being self-employed is too hard and does not bring any security? To connect to your deepest longings, you must open up to the idea/belief that anything is possible and help others do the same. I used to be a full-time professional singer. In 2001, I decided to take a break from singing and move into the speaking and training industry. Even though I understood and still recognized the transformative power of music, I didn't want to get stuck entertaining people just for entertainment's sake. I believed that I would be able to have a greater effect on people's lives through teaching personal growth. Later, when I would think about the music industry, one of my strong beliefs was that if I wanted to play music the way I liked to, I would have to put more time and effort into it than I wanted to. Also, the idea of just playing every now and then in a coffee shop or for an "Open Mic Night" to get back into it did not inspire me at all. Because of this limited vision, I did not feel the desire to return to singing for quite some time. One day, however, it struck me to give myself permission to expand my thinking about how music could be a part of my life. I asked myself, *What would I ultimately love to do with my singing if money and time were not concerns?* The vision that appeared was of me playing with a group of fantastic "easy-to-be-with" musicians on a beautifully lit stage as I talked about feminine empowerment between songs to an appreciative audience. It was that very vision that inspired the keynote concerts that I present today on feminine leadership and empowerment.

Ask these "Power Questions" to help open up to possibility; give yourself permission to dream and think big!

1. What would you do with the rest of your life if you always had 10 million dollars in the bank and knew you could not fail?
2. What would you do with your life if you had less than a year to live and 10 million dollars in the bank? What would be the contribution you would most like to leave the world?
3. If you could attract any and all qualities in an intimate partner and not have to compromise on anything, what would this person be like?

Expand your thinking. Create a larger vision of what you think is possible. Then, when you ask yourself, "What do I *really* want?" your head won't jump in as quickly and say, "You can't do that!"

Key #5: *Seek Supportive Peer Feedback*

Humans are empathetic creatures by nature—we can feel when someone is connected to their joy and when they are not. Because of this, other people can help us discern the difference between our true desires and our conditioned responses—they can feel the subtle changes when we move up or down our "Joy Meter." When you connect to your heart's desire, others feel your energy rise with more joy. If you intend to share something but it's really something you think you *should* want rather than something you truly want, your support person or group will not feel your energy elevate—even if you share it with confidence. Your energy will feel flat to the others in the room. Having others mirror back to you what they hear coming from your mouth and what they feel from your heart energetically when you share can be invaluable in helping you discern what it is you really want.

It's important to have people stand witness to what we want and support us rather than repeating unsubstantiated reasons why we can't have what we want. Most of us have heard too many of these for too much of our life, from our families earlier in life (or now) to negative people surrounding us now.

Your invitation for key #5 is to find at least one person you can call or see (in person) once a week, with the specific intention of sharing what you want in your life. Choose someone you respect and who you believe is a caring, intuitive person, don't just choose the friend you see most. Share with them the small things you want and the big visions you dream of. If you want more guidance on how to give and receive this kind of support, join us at an *Art of Feminine Presence* intensive. I'd love to meet you in person. You can find dates and locations at **ArtofFemininePresence.com**

Kelly's goals were to have more confidence, cure some health challenges that had started to appear, and to start building her own business empowering women and girls. She was not following through on any of the things she already knew she needed to do, so nothing was moving in the direction of her goals. When I asked her "What do you do to avoid feeling anger?" she looked at me with a puzzled expression.

"I'm not usually an angry person. My husband gets it when he really frustrates me, but no one else."

"What is your drug of choice you use to not feeling your feelings as the day winds down from my busy life as a mum and wife?" I asked.

"Wine. I've noticed I want it every night now and there is less being left in the bottle these days."

"What do you think would happen if you stopped drinking for a week in order to feel what feelings arose?"

"Gosh, that would be really tough."

She was starting to see how she had created a high-functioning person's addiction. Alcohol every night is a clear sign of avoidance. Busy people make it okay to partake in a drink at the end of the day, "to take the edge off" because they "deserve" it. It's an addiction that society accepts. What is buried underneath the buzz of the alcohol comes out in health issues, relationship issues, and motivation issues that deaden lives.

Kelly agreed to my challenge, and we talked about having a place in her house to go when she noticed cravings or challenging emotions starting to rise up. She would drop home into her womb space and feel the internal space of her body as the anchor to the present moment as she allowed feelings to arise. Discomfort or withdrawal symptoms almost always come before empowerment. For Kelly, a lot of anger arose with a lot of tears. On the other side of ditching the avoidance behavior, following her joy, and having others to support and witness her, she launched her business, become a professional speaker, and lost 70 pounds as she regained her health and happiness. That's worth some discomfort on the front end, would you agree?

Listening to your heart and following your joy is like turning your head to the side to check your blind spot when you are driving. It gives you the information you need to stay happy, safe, and heading in the direction you want to go. If your heart's not in it, you're not going to get to your destination very fast. No matter how logical your action plan is, if you think you *should* do something, it will not manifest if your heart longs to take a more creative road. This is why so many people focus on what they think they want, and do their affirmations every day, but it never comes to fruition because their heart and head are in conflict. Always listen to your heart, even if it is feeling sadness, anger, or loneliness. It has enormous control on the direction of your life, so you might as well listen rather than fight it. Your heart is your ally.

CHAPTER ELEVEN SUMMARY

In order to create the life you want, you must be aware of your genuine heart's desires versus what you think you *should* want. After all, if you cannot feel and acknowledge your desires consciously, you will not manifest them in reality.

A woman's blind spot is often caused by her fear of separation. This can be the reason we cut ourselves off from feeling many of our heartfelt wants.

There are five key practices that will help you discern the difference between your heart's desires and what you think you *should* be, do, or have:

Key #1: Pause before you habitually respond

Key #2: Feel your authentic feelings

Key #3: Follow the joy

Key #4: Expand your thinking

Key #5: Seek supportive peer feedback

If your heart's not in it, you're not going to get to your destination very fast.

CHAPTER TWELVE

AROUSE YOUR LONGING TO BE LOVED

It doesn't interest me what you do for a living...
I want to know what you ache for,
And if you dare to dream of meeting your heart's longing.
It doesn't interest me how old you are...
I want to know if you'll risk looking like a fool for love—for your dreams—for the adventure of being alive.

From "The Invitation" ~by Oriah Mountain Dreamer

If you slow yourself down from the ever-increasing pace of your life and remain still long enough to feel your heart, you will probably find pain there. That pain is from the desires you have disregarded for so long or have forbidden to arise at all. It doesn't take much to notice that women's hearts are collectively aching— aching for love, for attention, for appreciation, for physical touch, and for a safe place to rest and let go. And yet true freedom and power, as we will explore now, come not from pushing away our longing for love, but from experiencing it.

Whether they admit it or not, most women on the planet want an extraordinary love relationship. The feminine in each of us deeply desires to love and be loved unconditionally. She wants to open her heart and be claimed by a strong presence. In an intimate relationship, she wants her partner to witness all her downfalls while still honoring her as a beautiful, precious being. In a sexual experience, she may revel in a series of orgasms, but her deepest longing is for intimate communion. Even though we women value our freedom, our autonomy, and our time alone to do the work we love, our primary yearning is to be in close heartfelt relationships. This is partly why women generally stay in less-than-fulfilling relationships longer than men: We long for love.

Many women shut themselves off from feeling their desire to be in an extraordinary love relationship because the prospect is too painful. They don't want to be disappointed. It's often easier to stay with the status quo and not expect too much. There's a part in all of us that believes that when we desire change, dream bigger, and set our sights on what we truly want, we set ourselves up for possible failure. And this is true; you may not be successful in getting what you want. Failing at creating what we want can activate that part in us that feels disconnected to source energy, to God, and it's that feeling of separation from this powerful source that is terrifying to the core because it then means we are separate from everything. The problem here is that if you do not *feel* your deepest longings, you will never create them as a reality in your life. The Universe/Source/God responds to your daily *feelings*, which go hand in hand with your intentions and goals, rather than to affirmations that are void of emotion.

Change is scary. Many women choose to remain single and not engaged with dating, or in relationships that are less than great, because the alternative (allowing themselves to actually feel the type of relationship they want) is too uncomfortable. If we really honored our desires, we might have to do something significant, such as leave a relationship, in order to live the fulfilling life we want, and that is a frightening concept for many women.

It's not easy to leave a relationship or get clear on what it is you truly want. If this type of scenario is familiar to you, be very gentle with yourself. Don't beat yourself up, and don't make any quick decisions. If you are in a situation like this, do some internal reflection on what it is you want in a relationship, and how you want to express yourself in a relationship. Then, give yourself an honest appraisal of how you express, or don't express, this grand vision, and what it is you need to change inside yourself to be ready for a great love.

Don't just blame the other person; what part of the dysfunction is yours? You always have the opportunity to grow in the relationship you are currently in, and I believe nothing is more important to our human existence than that opportunity to grow.

MY THREE ATTEMPTS AT TRUE LOVE

David Deida describes a transformative path of three stages a woman goes through as she aches to feel loved. This concept has greatly influenced my work. I recall pivotal experiences in my life where I moved through these stages. Those experiences helped me feel my deepest desires for an extraordinary relationship, and I now create just that every day with my husband. I call them my three attempts at true love.

FIRST ATTEMPT: ***"I need to get the love from someone else."***
Most women first attempt to get the love they seek from a man. I did. My dating life began with the anticipation that one day I'd be standing opposite the man who claimed my heart and could offer the wild love I dreamed of. In my yearning for love, I often tried to mold myself into someone my dates would like, pushing my intuition aside in order to start or stay in the relationship. I did not make great choices in who I tried to attract, and they never lasted long.

Whether a relationship lasts a lifetime, a year, or a few weeks, there comes a day when a woman awakens from her Cinderella illusion and realizes she cannot rely on one person to give her all the love she desires. Whether in a relationship or not, she recognizes that one person cannot give her the attention or emotional support she needs, and that to live a fun and balanced life she can't put everything on hold waiting for the perfect relationship to come along. I remained stuck in my less-than-perfect situation with men for a while, but I finally allowed myself to feel the pain and dissatisfaction that resulted, and this propelled me into my second attempt for true love.

SECOND ATTEMPT: ***"I don't need anyone else because I give myself the love I need—so if we get together, let's have a completely equal relationship."***
My second attempt for love started when I vowed that I would give *myself* the love I had been trying to get from someone else. I spent a lot of time on this attempt. When a woman is in this phase, whether single or in a relationship, you will find her working on herself and her personal growth. She appears strong and self-sufficient, at least on the outside.

This was the time when I developed my masculine side and became economically and emotionally self-sufficient. This was the heart of my independent, tragic, romantic phase that I described earlier. I practiced my "no" to men who did not respect my independent nature and to situations that were not in my best interest. This was a better place to be, as it broke the patterns of previous dysfunctional relationships. At the same time, however, I had an energetic wall that guarded my heart and tried to protect me from getting hurt, and I was not being approached as much by men. I proudly displayed the bumper sticker on my red Toyota Celica exclaiming, "*Single and Loving It!*"—and yet, in hindsight, this was merely another effort to cover up my longing for love.

If a woman in this second phase does find herself in a relationship, it will be with a greater expectation of equality. She will expect her mate to support her career just as much as she does his and she will expect him to follow her decisions just as much as she follows his. She will expect him to have developed his feminine side and to share his more sensitive, nurturing side with her.

While this second attempt offered me much strength, there came a day when I realized that having to always rely on myself and my own masculine within me did not fulfill me either. *There must be more than this*, I thought. *Sure, I have greater self-esteem and respect from men, but where is the passion, where is the magic, where is the wild love I so desperately want?*

On the path towards this love, I did not choose to look back or revert to a dysfunctional relationship in order to get love, which at times I had rationalized was "better than nothing," but I also didn't move ahead much in my awareness of what that love was. Liberation came when I finally chose to look forward and make another leap in consciousness. Similar to the leap that took me from my first attempt to my second, when I connected with my pain and dissatisfaction long enough, it propelled me into my third attempt for love, which was the only way out of my dilemma.

THIRD ATTEMPT: ***"I don't need to keep giving love to myself. I am love. I rest in knowing I am a fountain of endless love. Relationship is an opportunity to give love unconditionally, without expectations of return."***

My third attempt for love started when I realized that in order to be consistently overflowing with the feeling of love, I must be that love myself. I vowed to be the vessel that divine love flows through, to the best of my ability, no matter what happened. When a woman is in this phase and something or someone hurts her, she stays open—there is no need to guard her heart anymore. She always expresses love in service to the world, through her smile, her words, her body, and her voice. This does not mean that she allows herself to be taken advantage of, or that she gives of her energy more than what's healthy for her. It does not mean that she lets toxic people invade her space. Rather, she includes herself at the center of the world she loves; she does not forget herself. She puts her own oxygen mask on and keeps it there before she puts anyone else's on. A person who is used to making choices from the first phase would think this advice crazy, but to a woman in the third phase it makes sense and is a healthy way to relate to others and to the world around her.

There is no easy ticket through the first two phases—it takes spiritual practice towards higher stages of consciousness and a commitment to stay open and be the embodiment of compassionate love. That said, be patient with yourself through these three attempts. Don't try to rush through them or pretend you are in an unconditional loving space when you are not.

EXERCISE #18

For a few minutes today, imagine that you are a "fountain of love." You have an unlimited supply of love rising up in you and overflowing all around you. Extend this love to everyone you see. It doesn't matter who it is—a little girl skipping along the street, a homeless man begging for money at the entrance to the highway, or your best friend—whoever it is, extend your love and appreciation to them. As you do this, you'll feel your heart and body physically fill up with energy that is so pleasurable you may not want to stop. This is what it feels like to live as love and not need anything or anyone to be any different.

Deida calls the leap from the second to the third attempt "the feminine crisis." It's not a pleasant place to be, but it is where spiritual evolution takes place. Deida says, "If she can allow herself to relax into her despair without protecting her yearning and wounded Feminine Heart, the yearning itself will reveal her divine nature. If she can allow herself to be absolutely open, without trying to fill the 'hole' in her heart with food, or talk, or intimate hopes, this dark hole will eventually widen to the size of the universe."

This description is not just a series of beautiful sentiments to me—it is my personal experience as well. The key to communion, connection, and love is to experience yourself as the embodiment of love, whether that be in an intimate relationship or not. To do this, you must become aware, moment to moment, of when you are physically or energetically guarding your heart, your body, your voice, and your emotional expression.

When you open, you may get hurt. When you drop your armor, you may get stabbed in the heart. However, it is the very choice to stay open and unguarded that is the fundamental feminine spiritual practice—learning to live as love, whether a relationship is gifting you or not, and loving, even when it hurts.

LOVE—EVEN WHEN IT HURTS

I stared, disillusioned, at the man I had thought I was going to spend the rest of my life with. "I want a man who looks deeply into my heart and soul and knows without a doubt that he wants to be with me," I shared. The person sitting across the restaurant booth was *not* that man—as much as I had wanted him to be. For once in my life, I had broken up with a man first. Even though I believed that perhaps no one better would come along, I was clear that I would no longer settle for less than what was perfect for me.

My chest physically hurt when he left the restaurant, and I made my way outside to get some fresh winter air. Behind the building was a secluded open field that beckoned me towards it; it invited me to release my emotions in its embrace. My nose was red and my hands numb, but my inner body was a fiery ball of anger. Why was I deprived over and over again of the love I saw everyone else having a chance at? I looked up at the mountains and the full moon that illuminated the sky. My heart was overcome with terrible pain as I screamed from the depths of my gut. Then, something switched in my head, and I heard a still, small voice say, *don't ignore the hurt—feel it, from the depth of your being.* I felt pain, I felt anger, I felt betrayed. I felt like someone had wrenched my heart wide open. I kept groaning, "*WHY?... WHY?...*

Why does love always leave me?"

I leaned into the grief. I didn't let my mind take over to worry about what this meant for my future. I just stayed open to the pain and to my heart's longing, desperately wanting to love and be loved by a strong man.

After what felt like about ten minutes of staying with the discomfort, I was suddenly overcome with a sense, first of peace, and then of deep love. For the first time in my life, I felt what it was like to meet my pain head on, with no resistance, and to move through to the other side. I allowed the pain to open me, physically and energetically, and I was filled with love. I felt love for myself, love for him, and love for all the men who had hurt me in the past. I felt love for the physical place I was standing in and for the moon and stars above me. Looking back, I see what an enormous signal I rocketed out into the universe

that night: "I want a love relationship that has it all!" Through my pain, I opened my heart, and the way I loved was never the same again.

EXERCISE #19

The next time you feel angry or frustrated, feel it rather than shutting your heart down. Stay open-hearted instead of contracting in fear. Keep your body open and your arms out to the sides, and breathe into all the corners of your lungs. ***If you have tears, let them flow, and feel your throat*** *opening as sensations from the emotions rise up. Stay with the physical sensations and not your "story" of the event that occurred to cause this feeling. Don't analyze why this is happening. When we stay open—when we do not physically contract—we can feel more deeply and let love run through our body.* ***The more we stay present to our energetic and physical*** *body when a negative emotion tries to engulf us, the easier that emotion will transform into authentic power and love.*

A NOTE FOR SINGLES WHO WANT TO BE IN A PARTNERSHIP

Have you ever been in the following scenario? You haven't given up on your dream per se, but you feel so tired of being discouraged and failing at past attempts that you don't even *want* to feel your desire anymore. It's too painful.

Elizabeth was in this situation with her desire to meet her soul mate. She wanted a strong, committed, emotionally available, handsome man. She was clear on what she wanted, but was not allowing the energetic connection to **her desire. That link is critical. Most people don't know how to reconnect to** their desire for love. She didn't. As she got up at the microphone at one of the trainings, I encouraged her to not feel the desire for the perfect man coming into her life, but instead have her focus on desire itself.

Desire is an energetic opening. When you desire sex what do you feel? A yearn to open. When you desire yummy food what do you feel? A desire to open to it before you even taste it. When you desire a warm bubble bath, what do you feel? A relaxation even before you dip your toe in. For twenty minutes, all I instructed her to do was to feel her desire for desire—in her body.

Waves of joy came, ecstasy came. She was courageous enough to not shut it down as other women were holding space witnessing this. It was an unforgettable immense experience for us all to taste the magnetism that was now pouring out of every cell of her body. She came out the other side of the process feeling such connection to the love she wanted—with no attachment. She kept repeating to the group, "I desire him to show up today. I am open to it happening right now." We could feel the energetic difference between someone saying that from lack and her declaring it from a place of desire and unattachment at the same time. After years of being single and having lost her belief in what she could manifest in love, she met her future husband within weeks.

Your desire doesn't come from your head. It's an energy you align with. When you do, things can happen very fast.

I know firsthand how hard it is to stay positive after years of being unwillingly single. Like me, you will probably have your moments where you dive into drama, anger, worry, and distrust. That's okay, just notice when you do. However, come back to the following three practices, and see if you can experience how they work together.

1. Continue to feel your deepest longing for the kind of relationship that inspires and supports you. Feel this in the depths of your heart.
2. When fear, worry, and doubt arise, stay connected to your physical and energetic bodies. Feel the emotions, but keep your body open. If you are not present to your body, you'll probably dive right into the emotional drama and get lost in it. Over-feeling and over-identifying with the emotion are just as disempowering as repressing it and not feeling it.

3. Trust that the universe is right now hand-picking the perfect partner for you, more suited to you than you have ever dreamed of before today. One day, you'll look back to this time and find it hard to connect with the pain because the love and passion you will be experiencing with your perfect partner will be so immense.

We will come back to these practices again soon. They are so important.

DON'T MERGE IN RELATIONSHIPS

Relationships can be a woman's greatest strength and greatest weakness. Your feminine essence naturally wants to commune and connect, but if taken too far it turns into an unhealthy tendency to lose your sense of self in relationships. All the personal growth a woman does in her second attempt for love—being more independent and better at satisfying her own needs—is critical in order to live with an open heart, because through this she develops boundaries. In his essay, *Integral Feminism*, Ken Wilber describes the typical pathological form of the male's desire for truth and autonomy as:

"...power over, or brutal dominance and rigid autonomy. The male does not want to be *part* of anything else (communion), he wants only to be the *whole* himself (alienated agency): he fears relationship and values autonomy. Likewise, the typical pathological form of female communion is fusion: the female fears autonomy and disappears into relationship, often destroying her own identity in the process."[04] I'll share more on this in the next chapter.

It's a constant practice for me to deeply connect with my husband, whose presence I am in for most of every day, and still have a strong sense of my own individualism. I have to remind myself constantly that, as much as I value his opinion and love teaching with him, I can always make the final decision on the direction my own work will take.

---

04 Wilber, Ken. Eye of the Spirit: An Integral Vision For a World Gone Slightly Mad (Shambhala, 2001), p 171

I love leaning into my husband as we walk hand in hand down the street, feeling my own energetic field separate from his. This might sound counter-intuitive at first, but having strong energetic boundaries actually allows you to open your heart more. I think of a strong energetic boundary like a protective balloon surrounding my body, or I imagine standing in the center of a "light globe." I imagine the outer rim of the "light globe" a little more than an arm's length away from my physical body. When I have this beautiful layer of protection and "stay home" in my lower body, I can open both my heart and my body because I know that I don't always have to be on guard.

You don't have to let everything and everyone into your physical and/or energetic space in order to hear them and connect with them. It's a misnomer to think that you have to merge your energy field with others in order to be really friendly and intimate. We've all had the experience of someone trying to be friendly and feeling like they are encroaching on our space. In truth, it's when you are more at home within yourself, when you have a healthy feeling of separation and are *not* fusing with another, that you can create greater intimacy with someone else. Two telephone poles have to be buried deep and strong in their place in order to hold the cable tight between them; if they are not rooted, the cable between them goes slack. It is the same in relationships. If both people in a relationship do not have a strong inner core and a deep sense of self, the relationship between them will not be strong. One way I remind myself to stay in my core is to slightly lean back when I'm talking to someone. This small shift reminds me not to jump out and merge with the other person's field.

Be aware of your tangible actions and decisions as well as the energetic way you fuse with another rather than communing as two individuals. When you naturally embody love in the third phase, you never lose sense of your inner core and boundaries.

EXERCISE #20

When connecting with someone else, it is important to stay focused in the center vertical core of your body. Practice this exercise in person with the next person you interact with.

- *Step One: Bring your attention to the center point of your womb space. As you talk to this person, stay focused on this point in your lower belly; don't try to energetically jump over to where they are. Rest back in this place in your body, and notice how the* ***communication shifts****. When you feel you've been able to stay in the center point of your womb space while talking, move on to step two.*
- *Step Two: Bring your attention to the center point of your heart area. As you talk to this person, stay focused on this point in your body. Rest back in your heart, and notice what it is like to communicate with someone from this place. When you feel you've been able to stay in the center point of your heart while talking, move to step three.*
- ***Step Three: Finally, with your imagination and attention, find the*** *center point of your head (the center point of your skull). As you talk to this person, stay focused on this point in your head. Don't try to energetically jump over to where they are. We jump out of our own head space when we want someone to react to us in a certain way, when we are concerned about what they are thinking. Keep your attention on your own head.*

The center points of your head, heart, and womb space are the three *easiest portals through which to come into the center vertical core of your body. Together, they form your "energetic telephone pole." When you are strong in your "energetic telephone pole" and your partner is strong in theirs, the relationship between the two of you is naturally strengthened.*

RELATIONSHIP ADDICTION

In the *Art of Feminine Presence* trainings, my husband Datta and I talk frankly about how to sustain an extraordinary relationship, and if single, how to prepare for one. We often hear women say, "I'm clear on what I want but have a hard time following through on what I know." It's true: The easy part is to make a list of qualities you want in a potential partner and to get clear on which ones are "deal-breakers." The hard part comes after that: It takes commitment to actually act on what you know, knowing that it may bring up loss or loneliness in the short term.

The Higher Power that supports you in manifesting an extraordinary relationship is waiting for your heart-wrenching scream that belts out, "I will not settle for a limited relationship—instead, I will *be* that love I seek!" Don't make the mistake of underestimating such an emphatic statement. That Higher Power is listening, and it is waiting for your clarity.

"What you do speaks so loudly
I cannot hear what you are saying."

~Ralph Waldo Emerson

If you continue to choose partners that are not good for you, or move ahead in relationships you know are not what you want, you must treat this pattern like an addiction in order to let go of it. Giving up choices like these can be just as hard as choosing to withdraw from an extreme physical addiction like drugs or alcohol. When an addict makes the decision to stop taking drugs, they first experience a period of immense pain during the detoxification period. Things feel much worse before they get better. Similarly, as you withdraw from a relationship that is not good for you, you too will experience more pain before things get better. And yet, you must have the courage to feel the discomfort before you can break through and reach the other side. You have to be willing to feel the depth of your pain and heartache before you can gain the strength to always follow your highest thoughts about love.

Moving through to the other side—where love and peace abound—is where you are headed. When heartache comes, say, "Bring it on!" When disappointment comes, declare, "I will not close down!" These are the mantras of a woman who is open both as love and for love. When you embody this kind of love, your relationships will flourish. If you are single, sooner or later a soul mate will find you. It's impossible for him not to, because the light that radiates from you is so bright that he can see it from wherever he is in the world. You will not need to search, you will not need to control the way you meet. You will not need to do anything. You will be like the beautiful maiden, relaxing in the middle of a field, enjoying the sun and the smells of spring, who attracts the most stunning butterfly to come to her and sit right in the palm of her hand. Just like that, you will be amazed at how love will find you.

CHAPTER TWELVE SUMMARY

The feminine deeply desires to love and be loved unconditionally. Be careful not to close yourself off from your desire for a deep, passionate relationship.

MY THREE ATTEMPTS AT LOVE

- **First:** I need to get the love from someone else.
- **Second:** I don't need anyone else because I can give myself the love I need—so if we get together, let's have a completely equal relationship.
- **Third:** I don't need to keep giving love to myself. I embody love.

Stay aware of which attempt you are making in your relationships. There is no easy ticket through the first two phases—it takes practice and a willingness to keep your heart open, no matter what.

Continue to feel your deepest longing for a relationship that can open you more than you can on your own. When fear, worry, and doubt arise, stay connected to your physical and energetic bodies. Keep your body open. If you are not present, you'll probably dive right into the old emotional drama and get lost in it.

Trust that the universe is right now hand picking the perfect partner for you, more suited to you than you have ever dreamed of before today.

Remember to stay home in your body, and don't merge with another in relationship. The stronger your core is, and the stronger their core is, the stronger the relationship will be.

Lyrics to the song **"Sweet Sister"** by Rachael Jayne Groover

Sweet sister, you've been holding it together for so long
Your independence protects you, from the fear you'll be always alone
You see, the pain of closing off a surrendered heart is the way you've
agreed to play your part
Sweet sister, you've been holding it together for so long
I know you, I've been taught the same way to keep things small
I know the power of a woman can be the most threatening of all
In a world that chooses leaders who cannot feel the beat of everyone on
lands we kill
I know I want to bury all the ways I keep it small
Like the way I compete for beauty and for love Can't we find a way to
walk as One?
Sweet sister, can you see how you have never let it in?
They said softness is weakness, your sensual essence a sin
The story is mistaken it must come undone through the opening of our
daughters and sons
Sweet sister, I can see why we have never let it in
Let it in, let it in, let the joy and love and passion of life come dancing in
And if he breaks your heart, takes your dream, walks away, or makes you
scream
If he leaves the game without a sign
It will be ok. I'm okay. I'm still here, standing here with my broken heart,
open wide.

CHAPTER THIRTEEN

"Vulnerability" is Not a Dirty Word

There can be no vulnerability without risk; there can be no community without vulnerability; there can be no peace, and ultimately no life, without community.

~M. Scott Peck

Do you know someone who always seems a little guarded? No matter how friendly they appear on the surface, there always seems to be a wall that prevents you from reaching their heart? Have you ever been that person? To embody the feminine essence, you must be able to drop the invisible armor that shields your heart and let the love of others penetrate you. You must be able to allow your heart to open wider. Rather than fearing your vulnerability, you are invited instead to see the power in it, the sweetness of it. In this chapter, we will explore ways to access our softer, more receptive side, and to experience how it feels to live with an unguarded and undefended heart.

Several years ago, I went to a seminar to learn how to move past my fears. I expected journal exercises, group work, and perhaps to share some of my biggest concerns with others. When I walked up to the registration table, however, I was handed a form to sign. Its ominous message read: "In this seminar you will be invited to walk over a fifteen-foot bed of hot coals in your bare feet. Sign this form to state that you are doing this at your own free will. You understand that your fire-walk may lead to serious injury and possible death." I innocently asked the man behind the table, "When *is* this fire-walk?"—presuming I'd have a lot of time to learn how to walk safely. "First thing today," he said. My heart dropped to my stomach.

Within hours, I was surrounded by 5,000 others awaiting their turn to try this death-defying act—with no quick exit in sight. Loud tribal drumming pounded my ears. The crowd chanted, "COOL MOSS - COOL MOSS," as the trainers had taught us— somehow, this was to put into our minds that we weren't really walking on hot coals but on a wet bed of cool sweet moss. *YEAH RIGHT!* The crowd parted before me, and there it was: A 15foot lane of scorching hot coals. In a few seconds, there would be nothing between those coals and the soft, tender bottoms of my feet. Questions sparked by terror spun in my head. *Would my naked, vulnerable feet soon be burned beyond recognition? Would I nose-dive and scar my face forever? Could I find a way to sneak into the line of those already finished without anyone noticing?*

Suddenly, the lane master firmly grabbed my shoulder, pointed upward, and, at the top of his lungs, yelled, "*GO!*" I braced myself, looked up, and stepped onto the coals. "*One – two – three – four – cool moss – cool moss – cool moss – cool moss –nine– ten – eleven – twelve – COOL MOSS – COOL MOSS – COOL MOSS – COOL MOSS…*" I did it! I had just walked over hot coals and emerged unscathed. I had moved through my fear, I didn't get hurt, and I was okay.

Six months later, I staffed the same event and faced those hot coals again. This time, I felt less frantic fear but more concern that I would burn myself. At the staff training, people had shared stories of how they had burnt themselves. This was not news I had wanted to hear. Right up until the last minute, I had debated whether I would take the walk again, but then the daring voice in my head had said, *Who are you to have brought eight friends here, have them walk, and you chicken out?* I had to walk, and I did. I thought of cool moss, pumped myself up, and took that first step once again. "*One – two – three – four – OUCH! — not cool moss, hot coals!*" It only took four steps for my brain to receive the emergency message from my feet—"*Get out of there!*" I hobbled off to the first aid tent as inconspicuously as I could, where I was greeted with a cold bucket of water and a caring coach to help me through my emotional process.

I tried to wrap my brain around the experience. What had I done wrong? Had I done something different this time that had made me burn my feet? The coach kneeled in front of me and shared words that are still with me today. "Whenever someone gets a 'hot spot' from their fire-walk, it is a gift. Be quiet for a moment and ask your higher self, what is the message for you in this experience?" She walked away to give me a moment to be with myself. In the silence, a clear message came. *I had moved through my fear—I DID get hurt—and I was* still *okay.* That was exactly the experience I had needed. Somehow, I had had it in my mind that the aim in life was not to get hurt. Even though it had *appeared* I was working to move through my fear, I was actually working very hard to avoid pain and rejection. This very mindset had held me back in business and kept real love at bay.

What are you *not* doing out of fear of getting hurt? Are you guarding your heart in some way? A fulfilling life includes getting hurt sometimes. The question is, *Can you stay open, loving, and unguarded, even when the pain comes?*

WHAT'S SO GREAT ABOUT BEING VULNERABLE?

How adorable is the vulnerability of a baby, a sweet little puppy, or a young child? We instantly fall in love with them. The same is true with adults. When we let another see our vulnerability, we let them into our heart, and they feel a deeper, sweeter connection with us. When I show you my humanity, it breaks down the imaginary barrier between us. If you've ever attended a personal growth workshop or retreat, you have probably noticed how easy it is to "fall in love" with the other people there. This is because when we share and witness another's imperfections and softer sides, we see we have much more in common than not.

In *The Awakened Speaker®* training I lead with my husband, people often ask us, "Doesn't it put people off when we share too much about ourselves?"

Great question! Vulnerability is not the invitation to air your dirty laundry or appear weak just to get sympathy. Rather, being vulnerable and open is sharing who you are underneath the façade. No one can relate to a perfectly polished speaker who doesn't share any of their personal foibles. When you share your vulnerability it allows those listening to feel intimately connected to who you are and what you say.

Many women shut down their vulnerability for fear of being criticized, put down, or teased as too "girly" or too weak to "play with the big boys" in business and life. Many people believe that a person who is emotionally expressive is not as powerful as one who can hold their emotions in and not let them show. But when we look at the facts, this belief doesn't prove to be true. People who share their feelings not only live longer, they have richer relationships, form deeper connections, and inspire more people than those who are cut off from the emotional realm.

Being vulnerable is a necessary part of opening to love and passion. The masculine essence has a natural desire to protect and provide for the feminine. Men have done this for millennia. It is a win-win situation, a good thing, not something that "keeps women in their place." Men are generally physically stronger than women and can therefore dominate us easily, so teaching our men and boys how to respect and take care of a woman ensures our safety and survival. Telling a young woman not to let a man open a door for her does not serve her. We need to support our young women to expect the men in their lives to protect and respect them, even while acknowledging they are capable of creating a great life for themselves. A woman who can hold true to her own power and at the same time allow a man to provide for and protect her will have more ease and joy in her relationships with men. A woman who always has her tough, "nothing is going to get to me" exterior, or her independent, "I have everything handled" exterior in place is simply not as attractive to a man. A masculine man enjoys providing for, protecting, and being "needed" by his woman. This is a win-win situation, ladies.

YOUR INVISIBLE ARMOR

The signal you send to others is either one of guardedness or openness—or somewhere in between. Your armor you use to keep you from feeling your vulnerability cannot always be seen, but it can certainly be felt by others. That armor makes it difficult for the world to know you are available for love, friendship, and joyful times, and it decreases your magnetic presence. One way to know if you have let your invisible armor down is to tune into how warm you are around men. For many women, it's a challenge to be totally unguarded around men. As I mentioned earlier, one of the qualities men seek the most in an intimate relationship is that of a woman's warmth. Men are attracted to warm, friendly, open women. This is different from "easy" women—think opposite of a woman who is a little hard around the edges. Often, women think of themselves as warm when, in reality, they are only like that around their cherished girlfriends.

Another way to check in with how guarded you are is to ponder how often you let others really listen to your deepest sharing. Those who have been hurt and have guarded hearts almost always steer the conversation back to the other person as a defense so that they don't have to share about themselves and be truly seen and heard. Does that sound familiar?

EXERCISE #21

Part 1 *– Below are a series of spectrums representing different ways you could be perceived by others. With the intention of gaining more awareness of how you are perceived, rate where you think you fall on each spectrum. We all move up and down on each spectrum, so don't judge where you are presently—just notice and pay attention.*

Friendly/Warm with the opposite gender who are *NOT* potential partners

Extremely — Average — Not at all

Friendly/Warm with the opposite gender who *could be* potential partners

Extremely — Average — Not at all

Guarded

Extremely — Average — Not at all

Sexually available/easy

Extremely — Average — Not at all

Ready for a relationship

Extremely — Average — Not at all

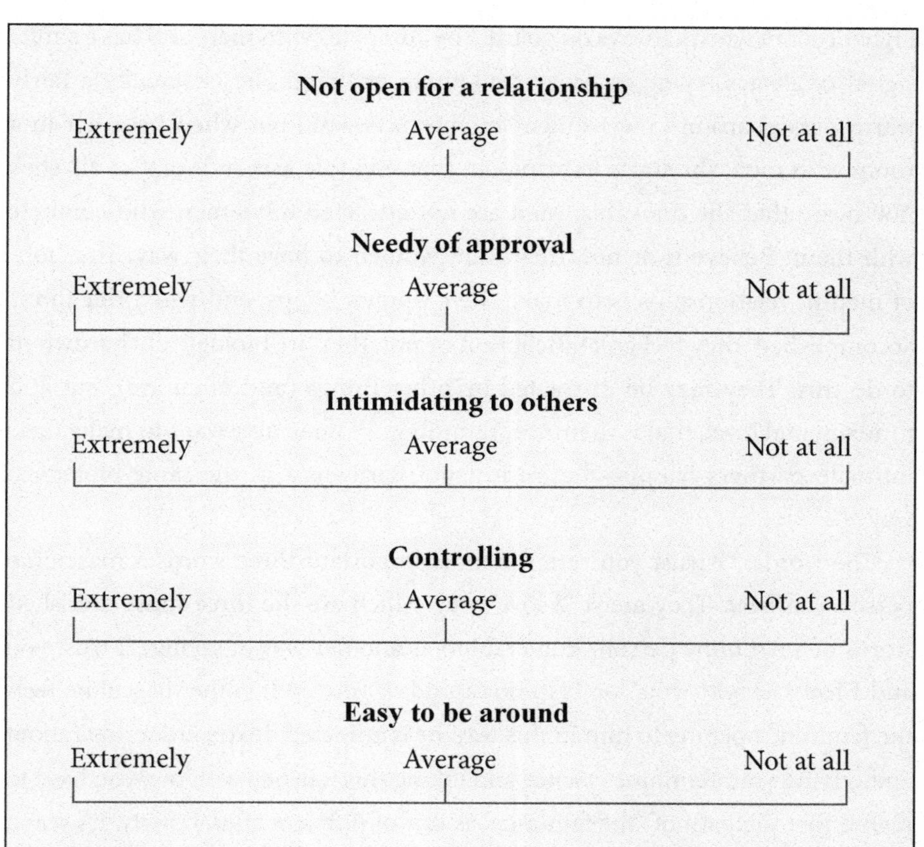

***Part 2** – Ask at least two trusted friends to give you some feedback as to how they perceive you on this continuum—without telling them where you consider yourself to be. Ideally, choose a friend from each gender. The best type of person to ask is someone who has known you for at least a few months, and they must have your best interests at heart. Don't ask a friend who you sense may be in competition with you in any way. The other challenge may be to find someone who is willing to be straight with you. You will get better results if you are very clear with this person that (1) you realize it can be hard to be totally honest when you know the friend you are being honest with may not totally like what you have to say, and (2) you appreciate what a big request this is and are grateful for their help.*

I have a client who is always on guard. She competes with men, and has a subtle signal of always trying to prove something to them. She is actually a fairly warm person around the women she interacts with, but when I see her in a room with men, she starts to bring out that invisible armor. Worst of all, she's not aware that she does this. Men are not attracted to women who compete with them. Believe it or not, they want women to have their way. The "job" of men in relationships is to make their women happy, and when this job is accomplished, they feel great. Believe it or not, they are biologically hardwired to do this. They may be distracted by other things (and often are), but at a fundamental level, that is their programming. Women also want to make their intimate partners happy—they're just not hardwired in the same biological way.

The words, "I trust you" are the most important three words a masculine person can hear. They aren't "I love you," which are the three most cherished words of a feminine person. Vulnerability is another way of saying, "I trust you and I feel safe with you," or, "I'm not afraid of you." When the masculine feels the feminine opening to him in this way, he is attracted. If you are serious about embodying your feminine essence and taking this journey with me, you have to realize that the path of "the feminine" is one of ultimate vulnerability. It's scary, and it's painful sometimes, but it's a powerful state to live in. When your heart is wide open, with no defenses—when not even the possibility of a knife through your heart can close you down—you are free to love and be loved.

It is often on the energetic level that our invisible armor shows up. The more any part of us is energetically open, the more love and support we can receive. If someone hugs you and you do not feel the love and support they give you, you are missing out on receiving what that person has to give. When you receive a compliment or an unexpected gift, you may say, "thank you" with a smile, but if you do not really let the moment "sink in" and feel the other person's love for you, you are not fully open to receive. When you share intimate moments with your lover, you may enjoy physical pleasure, but if you are not totally present to the love being exchanged, or the inner beauty in that person, you are not fully open to receive.

BE OPEN TO RECEIVE

Many of us have been taught that giving is more important, more "spiritual," more rewarding, more appropriate, and more gracious than receiving. However, this is exactly why many women feel dried up, stressed out, and are not attracting the attention or support they want. Learning to receive and allow others to nurture us is critical in our capacity to know love. It helps us keep our "tank" full so that we can continue to be of service to ourselves and to others. If our well runs dry but we continue to try to give, it creates resentment and illness. If I don't take enough time to relax or receive other people's help with things in my life, it will eventually show up in my body as stress or disease. Being open to receive allows us to be more real and vulnerable with others so that we can develop deeper and more honest relationships. We are much more likely to create what we want in our lives when we are open to the pleasure and joy of receiving.

I believed for many years that in order to be perceived as powerful I had to become a success on my own and not rely on anyone else. If a friend or partner offered to help with something, I had three stock answers: 1) "No, it's okay, I'll be fine," (2) "Okay, you can help, but what can I do to help you in return?" or (3) "Yes, I'd love some help," but afterwards I would feel twinges of guilt rather than gratitude for the support.

Early in our relationship, Datta and I went on a road trip to the Oregon Coast. The room had a spectacular view of the ocean and was very comfortable. But there was one problem: It was too cold for me, and the heating was not working properly. In the moment I made this complaint, Datta asked if I wanted him to take care of getting Maintenance to visit our room to fix the problem. My first reaction was a sigh of gratitude. "That would be great." My second thought was out of guilt— "You can do it yourself, Rachael Jayne—or at least you should offer to take care of it because he is fine with the temperature—you're the one with poor circulation." Datta noticed my moment of indecision, and before I could answer him aloud he was out the door and on the job. Looking back on my reaction later that afternoon, I took out my journal and wrote:

If I am honest with myself, I don't want to have to deal with fixing such problems, even if I'm capable. I don't want to have to be self-sufficient and only rely on myself all the time. Instead, I want to feel open to receive his offers of support. Why am I sometimes resistant to being supported by someone else? If I could have it any way, I'd love to be with someone who loves solving problems I don't. That sounds pretty nice to me, especially when he already knows and treats me as a capable woman...

Being stuck in my need for independence is one way I disconnect from my feminine essence. I can't say I'm *always* comfortable receiving support now, but I am definitely much better than I was in those early days.

There are many ways we can open to receive. We can ask for help, we can accept assistance when offered, we can harmonize our beliefs with the prosperity we want to create, and we can hold our body open to receive a hug from someone.

EXERCISE #22

Journal Questions *(Consider these questions deeply)*

- *Do your behaviors demonstrate that it is more important to give than receive? If so, where/from whom did you learn that?*
- *In what ways do you find it easy to receive from others?*
- *In what ways do you find it difficult to receive from others?*

RECEIVING AS A PATH TO HEALING

Serena was courageous enough to get up at the microphone during one of my trainings and admit she was stuck. She felt like a prisoner in her own body. With multiple major surgeries, a car accident, and severe chronic pain for the past ten years, in her words she was living in 'hell.' Like most people who've suffered years of chronic pain, she had tried almost everything and felt shame around not being able to get out of her situation. As she shared her story, her desperation for relief was potent. Emotional and mental pain is far more acute when crippling physical pain accompanies it. She shared that she'd almost given up on finding relief and had almost given up on her life with thoughts of ending it.

I saw her inability to receive. Her energy told me she didn't feel the Universe was on her side and it wasn't safe enough to relax her body. She felt she had to fend for herself even though rationally she knew she had friends who cared about her. Given that, I knew she would not be able to unwind the tension in her body on her own.

She decided to continue working with me after the event as a last hope. Some might say her recovery was miraculous. Serena and I now share that her liberation came because she became a better receiver. Twice a week we came together with a small group of women to witness her. She gradually found a way to not let the desperation take over, and found a place of non-resistance and relaxation with the pain so she could receive the 'aliveness' of the present moment. Physical pain can cloud our present moment. Receiving the aliveness of the moment means you can remain in the presence of your body so your fear that the pain will never stop isn't blinding. The pain just becomes sensation and presence.

The more weekly practice she did, the more she received guidance of what to do next, and the more she could feel relaxation happening, little by little. Through her intuition, reading some medical research that caught her attention, and attracting a more attuned health care provider, she realized things about her body she'd never understood before, which led to the chronic pain unwinding. A year later she was able to be on stage with me and share this incredible story; her smile bright, her body happy, and her celebration that she'd stumbled into a new business opportunity and a new man she was dating after years of being single.

The power of receiving is not just about receiving compliments with more grace or receiving more money. It's about receiving a higher power that knows how to get you through any challenge you face. Serena followed what she received. She practiced being in her body in a state of receiving, which unwound the pattern of always being on guard in every aspect of her life. Now she can receive all the blessings that the present moment allows for when she is in that space.

YOUR VULNERABLE HEART

Your feminine power is owned and expressed when you have the courage to feel the vulnerability of your heart. Similar to bringing your awareness inside your pelvis to inhabit your sexual essence, you can bring your awareness inside your chest to sense the internal space in and around your heart. The simple act of resting your awareness in your heart starts to lessen the guarding you may have.

Your heart center is the gateway to your emotions, which hold untapped power—it's not a sign of weakness or lack of spiritual discipline like you may have been led to believe.

There is a story about a Zen master whose wife had just died. One of the master's students was shocked to witness the master sobbing in his garden, especially after hearing many of his talks on the impermanence of life. "Why are you crying?" the student asked. The master answered, "I am crying because I am sad."

Growth is not about becoming aloof or getting caught in the New Age trap of always trying to be positive. My experience is that the more I evolve spiritually, the more sensitive I am to emotions—both my own and those of others.

The idea that being emotional (i.e., running your life by your emotions) is not a sign of strength and power is paradoxical. In fact, your feelings and emotions *do* run most of your life, whether you admit it or not. Have you ever felt a lack of confidence and as a result kept fumbling with your words? Or, on the flip side, have you ever experienced feeling very confident, happy, and in the flow, and in turn noticed what you said seemed to come from an "inspired" place? Emotion is why a young man in the slums of Chicago picks up a gun and aims it at someone's head. Emotion is what inspires someone to fast for

60 days in protest. Emotion moves us to get married, get divorced, sleep in for half the day, or bounce out of bed ready to "change the world." If we agree, then, that emotion creates action, we must learn to have our emotions work for us rather than against us. There are only a small number of people who have reached a high level of emotional mastery. These people consistently witness the emotions that are present in each moment, allowing themselves to fully feel them, and yet at the same time they don't allow their emotions to blindly captain their ship.

EMOTIONS VS. EMOTIONAL DRAMA

Emotions are good. They help us determine what makes us truly happy and fulfilled rather than what we think we *should* be, do, or have. They help release blocks and heal our bodies. They are a natural part of being human. We grieve, we feel outrage, we feel happiness, we feel hope, we feel bliss. *Not* feeling emotions is what gets us in trouble.

Grasping onto an emotion in the moment it wants to move through us also gets us in trouble. This is what leads us into emotional drama. Imagine your range of emotions like a flow of dynamic feelings moving past you from left to right. Imagine you can see them in front of your body. Some emotions are uncomfortable, some are peaceful, some are painful, and some are joyful. If I allow this flow to continue, I don't get stuck in emotional drama. I can just witness the emotions and feel them as they pass on through. But when I reach out and grab onto the emotion out of fear, righteousness, or a concern that I'm always going to feel this way, I get stuck in the emotion itself and it does not feel good.

Witnessing an emotion means watching it and sending it love and presence, as if it weren't you but an adorable little girl who feels deeply. Feeling an emotion means allowing yourself to experience pain, joy, or relief through your body. When I witness *and* feel my emotions in the present moment, I have thoughts or make comments like, "I feel sad right now," or, "I can feel frustration," or, "I feel constriction in my throat as I start to feel angry." When I reach out and "grab onto" one of these emotions, my thoughts change to, "This always happens to me," or, "What if I never get what I want," or, "I'll always be alone."

Staying present with emotions is easier said than done. Just this week, I hurt my back while at the gym. I have a history of a very bad back injury several years ago, with many months of physical pain and depression. As I felt the return of that back pain, it was all I could do not to fall back into my past memories or project my anxiety into the future and believe this would be my fate forever. I had to be focused and intentional not to reach out and grab onto the present emotions and have them turn into emotional drama. It was hard. I was aware of the part of me that wanted to give in to the negative emotions. After all, I deserved to feel overwhelmed with sadness and fear, didn't I?

A client of mine has been in a very difficult place in the week of my writing this. Over the past six months, she has felt a lot of loneliness and sadness about not having a husband and family of her own. She shared with me the other day that she had felt somewhat better and more positive until the moment she was asked by a friend to join them for Thanksgiving. This brought up emotions of sadness and loneliness, as it was a reminder that she was alone again at Thanksgiving.

It's okay to feel the sadness or loneliness that comes up in the moment. We all want to love and be loved by that special someone. Where it starts to overcome us, however, is when we project this experience into the past or future. The moment my client grabbed onto the loneliness she was feeling and projected it into the future, thinking this was how it could be for many months or years to come, she got stuck in it. When she projected it into her past and thought, "This is how it has always been," she felt the cycle would never end.

If you are single and struggle to keep your heart open and your spirits high in the belief that true love will find you, I encourage you to shift your perception just a little. Often, well-meaning friends and teachers will say, "You have to be okay with the idea that you will always be alone, and then love will find you. Once you are unattached it will happen." I would suggest something else. Rather than work towards feeling okay with a loveless lifetime, bring the power of acceptance into this moment—into today. You don't have to be okay that it will never happen, you just need to find a way to be okay that it's not happening right now. This takes you out of drama and allows the flow of emotions and experiences to keep moving. Today, can you be okay with the fact that what you want has not manifested yet?

STAY PRESENT

We do *not* have to cave in to our emotions by saying, "I just can't help feeling this way." It's time we learned how to both witness *and* feel the vulnerability of our hearts so that we can grow in our authentic power and not give in to emotional drama. It's hard, I know. The next time you feel a painful emotion, you will have a decision point. You can let the emotion flow through you as you witness it and feel it fully, or you can grab onto it and project it into your future or past. Which one will you choose?

When you remove your invisible armor and open yourself to receive more and experience the vulnerability and power of your heart, your life will flow in the direction you desire. In this state, you can stop pushing so hard to make things happen, as more will be attracted to you. You will feel lighter, and in turn your feminine radiance will glow much brighter. When you drop your defenses, there is always a chance you will be let down, and that you might get hurt. But which sounds more fulfilling: to live a life half-lived while being guarded *just in case* someone comes along and hurts you, or to live a full life with your heart wide open, with the mindset that if someone hurts you, you will just have your heart broken open even wider, with more room to love and be loved? When your next "fire-walk of life" presents itself, remember: Don't look down, try not to trip, and *know* that if you do get hurt, you'll *still* be okay.

CHAPTER THIRTEEN SUMMARY

The personal growth path of "the feminine" asks you to drop the invisible armor that shields your heart so that love can penetrate and open it even wider. It invites you not to fear the sweetness of your vulnerability but to see the power in it.

Your invisible armor will drop away, and more love, passion, and ease will be attracted to you when you become aware of when your body is energetically closed, and deliberately choose to open it.

Allow yourself to receive more from others around you.

Understand the difference between when you witness *and* feel the power of your emotions rather than getting stuck in emotional drama.

CHAPTER FOURTEEN

5 Mistakes Strong, Independent Women Make in Relationships with Men

---

When men and women are able to accept
and respect their differences
then love has a chance to blossom.

~John Gray

Many women doubt it, but attentive, honest, loyal, ethically conscious, masculine males do exist. They may be a rare breed, but they *are* out there. Some of them are married and treat their wives like the most precious thing on earth; they are committed to their purpose in life and believe that relationship is a huge opportunity for them to grow emotionally and spiritually. Others are in the dating phase; these men don't rush into bed with just any woman but rather have a clear intention of finding a woman who is much more than just a pretty face, one who will inspire them to be more. And still others are single and available! If you are single and don't believe this, I challenge you to change that limiting belief. What happens when you buy a new car? You start seeing that make and model everywhere, even though you may never have noticed them before. Men are no different: If you tune your antennae to the aware masculine man channel, you will start to notice them in the same places they have always been. Men like this are worthy of giving your heart to. They *can* be trusted.

There are five big mistakes strong, independent women often make in their relationships with men; mistakes which stop them from attracting and keeping a quality partner. Some people have judged this list of mistakes as an attempt to take women back to the dark ages. As we explore these five mistakes, keep an open mind. I will offer you some practical ways of communicating with the other half of our species that are based on understanding the masculine essence, which is different to the feminine essence. The more you can relate to what motivates the masculine, what fulfills him, and what keeps him committed, the more success you will have in your relationship with men.

MISTAKE #1: NOT APPRECIATING HIS MASCULINITY

Men have many gifts to give the world. They protect, they lead with direction, they focus on what they are doing and work hard, they fix things, they bring adventure to our lives, they make us feel feminine … and the list goes on. Women, unfortunately, often think men should be more like them and do not honor their masculine gifts.

Just as a feminine woman wants to be understood and seen for the beautiful being she is without having to "do" anything, a masculine man also wants to be appreciated for what he does, how he provides for others, and where he's going. To feel "alive" in his masculine essence, he must know his life's purpose and head in that direction with focus and determination. He wants to be productive and contribute to life through his actions. If you, as a woman, don't appreciate his masculine essence, it will either diminish in your presence or he'll simply pass you by—while you wonder, "Where are all the good men?"

WHAT YOU THINK AND SAY ABOUT MEN

All too often, I hear negative, snide, or back-handed comments made by women about men. We've all most likely participated in this kind of thing at some point in our lives, whether we're aware of it or not. Often, these comments are contained within jokes that pretend to be "all in good fun." But what we women often don't take into account is that, just as the feminine has been devalued in its own way, the masculine, too, has been effectively criminalized for what it offers. In some ways, women today are more guilty of negative remarks about men than the reverse because our society as a whole tolerates negative remarks about men more than it does about women. In some circles, in fact, it has become so common to hear negative comments about men that it even seems normal on the surface.

Become a "vessel of praise" for men. Whenever you come in contact with a man, think of what you most appreciate about his masculinity. Then *tell* him what you appreciate. To say aloud why you love his masculinity will get his attention in a very positive way, as men don't hear things like this very often these days. Do this every time the opportunity arises, without consideration as to whether you will gain something or not.

EXERCISE #23

Journal Questions:

1. *What are some negative or limiting comments or thoughts you've had about men—or the masculine—within the last few years?*
2. *What do you most love about men?*

MISTAKE #2: TAKING ON THE MASCULINE ROLE WHEN HE DOESN'T

Often, a woman will step into a masculine role because the man does not take charge of his life and his commitments. For example, if the man doesn't follow through with what he said he'd do, or doesn't make strong decisions, then the woman will step in, take action, and make the necessary decisions in order to get things moving, even though they weren't normally her decisions to make. If the man is wishy-washy about his direction in life, the woman might start to make more plans for both of them and become more controlling. It's a natural thing to do, granted—if no one takes the lead, then there is no forward movement. But try to resist doing this. Your man will not feel like he needs to be in his masculine essence if you are taking on his role. He might think you taking that role will make you happy. He will not feel the need to step up, take charge, and treat you as the beautiful princess or queen you are if you are trying to do what you think he should be doing. And ultimately, he will resent you for this and nobody will be happy.

The good news is that you do have an alternative course of action. Rather than you being the masculine one in the relationship, inspire *him* to be in his masculine. Here are some ways you can do that:

Let him know how much you trust him and his decisions. This is as nurturing to a man as it would be to tell a woman she is beautiful and adorable, or that whatever emotions she has are okay and appreciated. When a man knows you trust him, he is much more likely to create a strong container for you to relax into your feminine. Every day, tell your man one specific way that you trust him, and watch his masculine side grow. The end result will be that you will find it easier to trust him, and an expansive cycle of growth will occur between the two of you. It's good to remember that we all tend to grow into the expectations people have of us—both positive and negative.

Pose a problem he can solve. This works much better than instructing him or resenting him for not "picking up" on what you want and need. Men love to solve problems, whether we want them to or not. By giving the man in your life a problem to solve, you will both be happy. One way to do this is to express your needs and desires as a problem. For example, if you want him to take you on an adventuresome date, don't just tell him where you want to go; instead, share how you would like some more spontaneity and fun in your life, and ask him if he has any ideas of what you could do together. Give him some idea of the things that would feel fun and spontaneous—after all, you need to make it easy enough for him to win this challenge you have set—but give him freedom to find his own way of making you happy. Remember, men love to make their women happy. Just don't make it too hard for them.

Be in your feminine. When you are in your feminine essence, you inspire your man to connect to his masculine essence. Everything written in this book is geared to help with this very endeavor. Be open to more ways that will help you *not* take on the masculine role.

MISTAKE #3: NOT REALIZING THAT A MAN WANTS A WOMAN WHO INSPIRES HIM "OUT OF HIS HEAD"

We've heard it said time and time again: "Men are only after one thing." But is this true? It's true that men put a woman's sexual attractiveness high on their list of priorities, and that they are biologically programmed more than women to be driven by sex. But at a deeper level, what a man really wants from his woman is to be inspired "out of his head."

Most men live in their heads much of the day, and that's part of why the feminine is so captivating and relaxing to them: They have a deep inner need to let go of their incessant mental activity. Sex satisfies this need very well, although there are other ways a woman can offer this gift too. The way you talk, move, and relate can either invite a man "out of his head" or keep him stuck there. Express how you *feel* more often than speaking intellectually.

When you walk and dance in a sensual way, it inspires him into his own body. Don't think you have to intellectually stimulate a man to attract him. It's true that that is part of any quality relationship, but it's not what primarily attracts men.

Jeff and I had a mutual spark of attraction the instant we met. We had a lot in common—a lot of love and a lot of passion—but very soon into our dating relationship the sparks started to disappear. Jeff was highly intelligent, an articulate man many years my senior, and so I wanted to "meet him" intellectually. He would talk with me about his work or the projects he was contributing to, and I would then feel compelled to teach him about what I was doing. It made me feel smart that I could offer him as much as he offered me, and I assumed this was what he wanted. The problem with this was that masculine men like Jeff are fed more by feminine offerings in an intimate relationship than by masculine offerings.

It wasn't until after my relationship with Jeff disintegrated that I realized that I had used my intellect and played the role of teacher to keep myself safe and out of my vulnerable feminine. In subtle ways, I would revert back to my masculine direction and intellect so I could feel somewhat in control—versus staying emotionally open and sensually expressive. This had not inspired him "out of his head."

Don't choose a man you think you need to teach, or a man you think you can change. You can teach other people, other men, but not your intimate partner. Trying to change anyone, when it is not invited, is almost always a waste of energy. A wise woman I know, who has long been an expert teacher on the subject of relationships, recently found her beloved. When he expressed interest in learning about relationships from her, she sent him to learn from another teacher that she highly respected instead. She did this because she fundamentally understood that if she were to teach him it would set up a dynamic that would diminish the sexual attraction between the two of them, and that would be hard to undo.

I am *not* saying you should never share things with your man, teach him about things you know, or discuss philosophy with him, but depending how far and deep you go in those discussions, know that these may end up decreasing the sexual polarity in your intimate relationship. Don't hide your brilliant mind from any man, or play dumb just to make a man feel good about himself, but do remember that the gifts the masculine male longs most for are the ones given from your feminine essence.

MEN ARE ATTRACTED TO LIGHT

Think of the feminine as Light. Men are attracted to Light like moths to a flame (not that I wish any harm to men). This Light is a woman's radiance, and it comes through her voice, her body, her smile, her hair, her skin, and her personal offerings, which can be anything from a meal, to a poem, to a dance, to the colors she wears.

As a general rule, if a man is not focused on his work, his attention will be drawn to the brightest light in the room—literally. If you wish to gain a man's attention, you have to be brighter than the TV, the computer, and other

Light-filled women. This subject may hit some sore points for you; whether you gain or don't gain male attention because of your looks, either experience can be hurtful. If you are not a traditional beauty, it's true that you may have to work a little harder for immediate attention, but the good news is that much of your magnetic pull comes from you feminine essence—it's a much more even playing field than you might have thought.

You do not have to be the prettiest woman in the room to gain the attention of an aware male, but you do have to have your Light turned on. A woman cannot always dress in sweat pants and expect a man to come knocking on her door in search of her feminine radiance. Neither can she always wear a grey business suit with her hair tightly bound and expect to stop traffic. Similarly, a man cannot sit on the couch drinking beer with no purpose and expect a powerful *and* feminine woman to want to be part of his life.

One of my clients recently asked me, "Can't I ever relax and be loved for *me*? Why is there always the pressure to be beautiful? Don't men just commit at some point?" Great questions! But I don't see "keeping my Light on" as pressure, I see it as pleasure. It's not that you always have to look your best to please a man; you can relax and be yourself too. In fact, when you relax and experience more play and joy, your feminine essence is more alive. You will actually be given more attention when you have a relaxed body and mind, as that is very attractive to a man who is hardly ever relaxed.

The following are some tips on inspiring your man "out of his head":

Soften your body. I place my focus on my belly, heart, and throat and soften them. I breathe deeper, and with each breath I relax and release as much tension as I can from my body. In that moment, he feels the shift in me and becomes more present to me.

Speak emotionally rather than intellectually. When I ask Datta how his work is going, I ask the question from a feeling place rather than talking about his to-do list. I might ask, "How are you *feeling* about working with so-and-so," or "Is there anything you could do to make your work day more enjoyable?" To answer these questions, he has to get in touch with what he wants to feel rather than remain in his head.

The power of touch, both sexual and non-sexual. A sweet caress or kiss is an obvious way to inspire a man into his body. Make sure you touch your intimate partner often. Affection is critical in a loving relationship, but make sure there is plenty of touch that neither of you thinks has to lead to sex. Use touch intentionally, and have it be a good mix of both sexual touch and compassionate, friendly affection.

Flirtatious looks. When Datta looks deeply into my eyes with a penetrating gaze full of love, I almost lose my balance. It is precious and inspires me out of my head immediately. The same goes for Datta when I give him a flirtatious or deeply loving look. Use your eyes as a tool to inspire!

Wear something beautiful. Colors, beauty, texture, cleavage, bare skin . . . all of these inspire a man out of their head. Need I say more?

There are many other ways you can inspire a man out of his head; these are just a few. Think about some ways you already do this with the men in your life. Don't fall into the trap of thinking beauty is superficial. Beauty can help us be more present.

MISTAKE #4: THINKING, "I DON'T NEED A MAN"

When I was in the college dating scene, I noticed two types of girlfriends (in relation to boys and men): The "low-maintenance girlfriend" and the "high maintenance girlfriend." My best friend, Fiona, and I would joke frequently about where we fell on that spectrum. I prided myself on being at the lowest point of the "low-maintenance girlfriend" spectrum, while she was on the higher end. To me, being a "low maintenance girlfriend" made more sense because I thought it would get me the man of my dreams. I thought men didn't want to have to buy their girlfriends gifts, or give them a lot of attention, or be there for them every time they had a problem. But that plan did not seem to get me very far.

Years later, while sitting in my office one day, the realization suddenly hit me: I want this office full of beautiful flowers from a romantic man. I want a man who will bring me lunch on a busy day. I want someone who will love me, romance me, and shower me with unique gifts—not someone who is okay with my not asking too much from him. I want to be a "high-maintenance princess!" I had originally thought that if I wanted too much it would push a man away. Today, however, now that I understand the masculine and feminine essences, I know that what a man wants is to give to a woman, and that if he doesn't have a sense of being needed his masculine isn't honored and he is not attracted.

Was it true that what I really wanted was a man to "take care of me?" I faced facts and came up with my honest answer—YES! Not in a way that made me feel helpless, but in a way that I didn't always have to do everything myself.

Men put most of their attention on what is needed, which is why many bright, self-sufficient women are caught in an unfortunate Catch-22 situation. The culture of the last 50 years has taught women to set their lives up so that they do not need to depend on anyone else. But the essence of the masculine is drawn to women who need them. Men prioritize what is needed so they can be more efficient in problem solving and getting things done. During the courtship period, the man makes giving attention to the woman a high priority. He wants to woo her, and so attention is needed. The challenge comes in years later, when wooing isn't necessary, at least in the man's mind. As time passes, the priority he places on giving his woman attention starts to fall lower down on the list, as he has already won her heart. This phenomenon causes a lot of pain in relationships, as women continue to need a lot of attention. But this pain can be lessened. Practice, as the woman, not taking it personally, and remember your man has a priority list. Without nagging and demanding his attention, create things you want and need him to do, and ask for them directly and often. Don't presume that he should put you as number one all the time, and don't presume he can read your mind with what you want.

If a man does not perceive that he can be of service to you, he won't be attracted to you. This does not mean you must play the damsel in distress, or be a nag, or be "needy." Men want to be free and autonomous, *and* they want to fill a need. Don't be demanding. If you say to yourself, *I need a man to feel whole and complete*, that is too big of a need for a man to fill. Aware men will be repelled by that, instinctively knowing that it's impossible to fill. Start creating smaller needs and requests, not demands, and see what happens.

Below are some examples of small ways you can create openings for men to step in—but watch your level of attachment to how he responds. These things are *not* intended to manipulate men. Just stay curious as to whether he wants to "fill the need" or not, and honor what he chooses.

- Give him a chance to open doors for you, and don't make a big deal about it, whether he does or not.
- Let him carry your bags—again, not making a big deal of it.
- Let *him* find something to do for the evening, after telling him you want to do something fun together.
- If you feel emotional, share that. Let him hold you or just listen to you. Feel free to ask nicely for *exactly* what you want.

Always remember that the difference between asking and demanding is that asking has no expectation that the other person must meet the request. Be open to "needing" a man. Stop playing the role of Super Woman who does everything herself—even if you *can* do everything yourself. What if the greatest sign of strength were to let go of control and allow someone else to help you?

EXERCISE #24

Make a list of all the ways you "need" a man in your life. "Need" has a different energy than "want." I am using the word "need" intentionally. If you cannot come up with 5 needs easily, this chapter will be a good one for you to keep referring back to. Keep asking this question throughout the day until you come up with 5 ways you "need" a man.

Mistake #5: To not deliberately create sexual polarity

In Chapter One, we talked about how when the opposite poles of a magnet face each other they create a strong, attractive force. Many women tend to gravitate towards the middle of the continuum as they develop their masculine sides in order to cope with today's socio-economic environment. Men, too, tend to move towards the middle, under social pressure to develop their feminine sides and not be so "macho" and dominating. The result of this is that many couples experience a lack of passion in their relationships, or, if passion is there in the beginning, it fades quickly.

A crucial relationship skill is to deliberately create sexual polarity by connecting to your feminine essence—at appropriate times. There may be times in the day when you do not feel very connected to your feminine essence and may not need to be, such as when you pay bills or write a shopping list. On the other hand, there may be other times of the day when you really *want* to connect to your feminine essence, such as when you lie in bed with your lover, while on a romantic stroll, or after a tough day of work.

A woman who can attract and keep an extraordinary relationship is aware of where she is on the sexual polarity continuum, particularly when she is around her intimate partner. She chooses to move towards her feminine essence as much as possible, especially at appropriate times.

The most important times to connect to your feminine essence are:

- When you are getting ready to go on a date
- When you and your lover spend quality time together
- When you are transitioning from your work day to your evening
- When you first get up in the morning
- Just before you go to bed at night

EXERCISE #25

Look at the continuum below, and plot on it where you think you are <u>most</u> of the day. Remember, we move back and forth on the continuum, depending on what we are doing, so just have a guess as to where you are on average.

Very masculine	Neutral	Very feminine

Then, ask a trusted friend (one who sees you in person often) where they see you on the continuum—without telling them where you consider yourself to be. Then, figure out one thing you can do that will move you one step closer to the feminine end of the continuum. Don't expect to make a huge leap, just practice consciously moving towards your feminine essence.

Warning! This power of attraction is so strong that it can get us into trouble. When attraction based on sexual essence is present, we may mistake it for "having found our soul mate." This is not necessarily true—it is just sexual attraction. I have observed this time and time again when I coach women. They feel this almost overwhelming attraction and mistake it for God's voice saying, "He's the one." Always question your first impulses—they may be right, and they may not be.

Now that you are aware of the five biggest mistakes strong, independent women make in relationships with men I invite you to turn them around by experimenting with the following five practices:

1. Appreciate men and their masculinity. Become a "vessel of praise." Verbalize your appreciations as often as possible.
2. Resist taking on the masculine role, even when your man does not step up. Instead, inspire (not manipulate) him in his own masculine direction. Men know when we are manipulative. It may not always be a conscious knowing, but they know.
3. Learn and try out ways to inspire men "out of their heads." They want our feminine offerings to be our gifts to them. Try this with friends. Always respect the other's boundaries, but notice how well it works—even if it's very subtle.
4. Become more open to receive from men. Allow them to give to you without your thinking it somehow reflects on your strength or independence. Express sincere gratitude when they do.
5. Become a deliberate creator of sexual polarity, and bring out your feminine essence when it is called for.

These five new behaviors will alter the way men respond to you. If you are a little put off by any one of these, just be open to testing it for a few weeks. You will notice the attentive, honest, loyal, ethically conscious, masculine male being attracted to you—as a friend, and as a potential mate, if you are available for that. Look around for this rare breed, and have fun picking them out of the crowd.

They are truly beautiful to witness.

CHAPTER FOURTEEN SUMMARY

The five mistakes strong, independent women make in relationships with men—and practices to change them—are:

Mistake #1: She does not appreciate his masculinity.

Practice: Be a "vessel of praise" for men, especially when they are in their masculine essence.

Mistake #2: She takes on the masculine role when he doesn't.

Practice: Inspire him to take on the masculine role—resist the need to jump in and take it for him.

Mistake #3: She does not realize that a man wants a woman who inspires him "out of his head."

Practice: Turn your Light on in all ways and remember, the masculine is attracted by your feminine gifts.

Mistake #4: She thinks, "I don't need a man."

Practice: Find small ways that you can create "needs" for men to fill.

Mistake #5: She does not deliberately create sexual polarity.

Practice: Remember, there are important times of the day where your feminine essence is called for.

CHAPTER FIFTEEN

The Dark Side of the Feminine

We cannot change anything until we accept it. Condemnation does not liberate, it oppresses.

- Carl Jung

There are aspects of your personality that are easier to accept and express than others. For example: loving, funny, generous, and intelligent might be qualities that would fall into the category of being wonderful to claim. We've been told hundreds of times that these are good qualities to have. There are other qualities we tend to reject and don't want to express. Angry, bossy, greedy, and needy might fall into this category for you. These are qualities we've been told are bad.

When messages come at an early age and are reinforced from different people, we decide at some level that we should do all we can to express certain parts of ourselves and not others. The problem is that we have all aspects of humanity within us. We are independent and dependent; we express love and fear; there are times we are aggressive and passive; defensive and open; patient and impatient. We have access to both ends of these spectrums and every quality serves a purpose and has a life-affirming role to play, if that quality is used consciously at the right time.

When we don't acknowledge and have compassion for a quality we don't like, we try to force it out of our lives. That's when the trouble starts. The parts that get hidden away from the conscious mind are still present. It's just that they are now in the unconscious mind so we don't have power to use those qualities how and when we want. They have power over us. When parts of your personality move to the unconscious realm you don't have an emotionally-mature connection with them. Imagine a young girl being told to go to that corner and shut up. After being ignored for a while, she is going to get angry and demand some attention. Those repressed qualities want to get our attention so they can become an integrated part of us.

The qualities that we deny are referred to as our "shadow" aspects in Jungian psychology. They are the parts of ourselves that are out of view in the darkness of our unconscious. They are blind spots that stunt our growth. These qualities that we relegate to the shadows are not always negative qualities; they can be positive qualities too. Has it ever been hard for you to own that you are beautiful, inspirational, sensual, intelligent, or wise? Negative qualities I refer to as dark shadows and positive qualities I call light shadows.

Our dark shadows do not usually get our attention in a healthy and productive way. Here are several ways your shadow can show up in your life.

1. It shows up in a sudden forceful blast and you cannot control it. When you are emotionally triggered, up comes your shadow. It could be a needy little kid energy or a passive-aggressive energy. It's that feeling of losing your rational, resourceful state—and something more emotional overtakes you.
2. Other people comment that you are the quality you are trying to suppress. You don't know why they say it, because you can't see it, but it sneaks out in unhealthy ways and they are on the receiving end.
3. Other people around you may express this quality, which usually irritates you. When it's hard to have compassion for how someone else acts and you get emotionally triggered by how someone else is behaving, it's almost always an indicator of your own shadow.
4. You have the brakes on to living courageously expressed and are having trouble manifesting what you desire. Every shadow quality has a virtue in it. The energy is useful. Angry, irresponsible, and selfish are all useful at times. If you shun them it shuts down your ability to be seen and heard and to receive what you want.

5. You have low energy and are not easily motivated. Every time you integrate a shadow back into your conscious realm you reclaim more of your life force. This is because you are not using your energy to try to push parts of yourself away. You have made peace with all of yourself and that allows you to be more present in the moment and in turn have more energy freed up.

THE COLLAPSE OF A WOMAN'S POWER

There are shadows common to women that have us easily collapse under pressure or show our darker underbelly. If we do not clean this up by looking at what we *don't* want to look at, no matter how much we wake up spiritually, our shadows will not disappear. You can wake up to the true nature of your spiritual essence, and you can deeply embody your feminine essence, but if you don't clean up your shadow material, you'll live with a static frustration under the surface that is trying to discharge, usually at others. Not a great recipe for great relationships, inspiring leadership, and being seen in the way you want.

I have a male client who is a couples therapist, one of the beautiful men I've worked with in our speaker training. He constantly hears from women who are not happy with the communication levels from their male partner. They complain they don't feel heard or appreciated, and they don't think their male partner is as conscious as they are. My therapist friend also sees another pattern that seems important for a woman to acknowledge. He explains that when the couple finally get to a place where the man feels safe enough to open up, and he finally starts to express his feelings and brings out what is under the rug, the woman often cowers or tells him why he shouldn't be sharing the way he is. Or that he shouldn't be sharing at all—even though that was exactly what she was asking for. The conversation becomes more confrontational as the man shares his voice, and many women don't like that. Dysfunction in relationship goes both ways. Men also very much want to be in a strong, healthy relationship.

How much confrontation can you handle until you collapse? The collapse of a woman's power can happen by getting smaller in her body, not speaking her truth, dispersing her energy so she's not really present in the room, getting overly emotional, and other generally unconscious tactics. For a woman to not shrink from confrontation she must work on feeling a grounded, localized, contained sense of self. Otherwise people can rattle her too easily.

As women embody their feminine essence, what is just as important that they get a stronger backbone. In a gross way we hear, "grow some balls" when someone needs to get stronger. Instead of this crass statement, what if we used "find your teeth." Teeth are there to growl and to bite. Both are important aspects of the dark feminine shadow. We've been taught not to growl (get angry) and not to bite (be nice). But if this remains a shadow and we can't harness our anger, it will show up in passive-aggressive ways. We can blame others, when it really is our own power that we have not solidified.

When shadows are left unexamined, our strength diminishes, we forget our desires, and give too much. Therefore we are not heard and valued, so we get angry and resentful because we don't get what we want—which rarely works.

Common Feminine Shadows

Here are the key shadows I believe women most need to own to embody true power along with their femininity, otherwise her ugliness shows up. At first you may think, "why on earth would I want to be any of these qualities?", but keep in mind every aspect of humanity serves a purpose.

Competitive

For the feminine woman the message has been don't be competitive, be collaborative. Being competitive is less evolved than finding middle ground and allowing everyone to win. But competition makes us better. It's the energy of improvement, motivation, and reaching our greater potential. When you excel at something you increase your self-worth and self-esteem. When I see someone doing better than me, I want to do better.

When the energy of competitive goes back into the shadows it turns into the dark side of the feminine. Women get competitive with other women, but behind their backs. Gossip, cattiness, tearing other women down is what it frequently looks like. The feeling of not being the best drives us to battle with other women for the little love, attention, money, fame we believe we can get. The battle is not out where it can be seen, but is hidden behind the backs of others.

In the shadows, the healthy energy of competition can turn into a lack of motivation. Lethargy, laziness, and self-forgetting tendencies take over because it's not good to try to be the best. "Just be like everyone else." "Definitely don't beat the boys." "No one likes a show off." Any of this relate to you?

Authority

For the feminine woman, the message has been "don't be too authoritative and bossy." It's not very lady-like. But being comfortable as an authority allows you to get your message across. It has people stand at attention and hear what you have to say without apology. It's the energy of leadership. In the shadows, the healthy energy of authority and owning that we are superior to others in certain areas, turns into arrogance and making others wrong.

The dark side of the feminine has criminalized the masculine. If you don't claim your authority consciously you will unconsciously tear down who you have felt has been in that role. I have often heard sentiments like "Males have created all the mess in this world." It's almost always said behind someone's back. When a woman's authority is in the shadow, her magnetic presence is significantly decreased, her voice is not heard, and the collapse of her power can happen in an instant. Any of this relate to you?

Needy

Women who grew up during the second wave of feminism in the 60's and 70's or had mothers from that era got the message that it was not okay to be needy. Don't rely on a man for happiness, or to provide for you financially or emotionally.

It's understandable to not want others to think you're needy, as it's not an empowering stance. But the energy of needy opens you up to receptivity.

Someone in need attracts others to help them. For those that push the 'needy girl' into the shadows, they often don't allow themselves to receive. They are always over-giving which can grow into a festering bed of resentment. Needy is the energy of vulnerability. Healthy vulnerability promotes receptivity too. Sometimes women whose shadow is needy have a hard time attracting a loving partner who wants to give to them and treat them like the queen they are. Men are attracted to that which is needed, therefore strong, self-sufficient women are in a Catch-22 situation in this respect. The dark side of the feminine turns vulnerability into an unhealthy display of never feeling like they can really do what they want unless others help them. When they don't get the help they want, the finger of blame rises and points to the closest person to her and says, "you are not giving me what I want." Any of this relate to you?

Selfish

For almost every woman the message has been don't be greedy. Consider others first. Everything doesn't revolve around you. Being selfish is not attractive. But the energy of selfish allows you to put yourself first, because if you burn out you will be no help to anyone. If I am selfish I give myself permission to look after myself well. I take time to meditate, to exercise, to eat well, and to be creative. If I put selfish into my unconscious with the fear that someone will think I am egotistically self-centered, it turns unhealthy fast. There is an epidemic of women over forty who don't put themselves first, second, or third. I can't even begin to count the amount of times I've heard from a woman at an *Art of Feminine Presence* training something like "I feel like I can't go for my dream career because I have to be there for my partner, kids, or aging parents." It has been heart-wrenching at times. I understand that there will be times that someone is in great need of your support, but you know when it's always that same story or just a one-time occurrence. When you fear being seen as greedy you don't have the power to attract the resources that you need. You'll be scared to ask for what you are worth in your job or business, sometimes you won't be able to feel what you are worth to determine that. When you fear people will think it's 'all about you,' you will make your voice less important. When you disown the energy of selfish you turn your feminine power into feminine weakness. Any of this relate to you?

Victim

For a woman committed to her personal power, the message has been to not act or talk like a victim. We are told, "You are not a victim, you create your own reality and must take responsibility for what happens in your life." But if you accept that sometimes there are victims, you can acknowledge that not everything is your fault. Women tend to take on other people's indiscretions: "It must have been my fault." We apologize ad nauseum. Women over-process with the question, "Why did I create this?" We weaken ourselves when we make it okay that someone else has done harm to us or someone else. I'm not saying always be a victim, but the dark side of the feminine takes it all on as her fault. That has to change.

When we push the vulnerable parts of us away into the shadows, we can unconsciously create situations where we are the victim. The energy of a victim doesn't feel safe in the world and they are unsure why. Give some attention to the part of you that has been hurt by others, and don't blame yourself for it. Any of this relate to you?

Perpetrator

The flip side of the victim is the perpetrator. The one who does harm to others. Most women hold men as the perpetrators, but we have all done harm to another at least a few times in our life. No one escapes this. Of course we don't want to live our life in a harmful way, but if a woman doesn't come to terms with her ability to do harm if needed, she will never create consistent secure boundaries in her life. She will not scream no when she needs to or protect herself and others when she needs to. The dark side of the feminine recoils with the fear of conflict. She doesn't speak up because she doesn't want to offend. She doesn't want to hurt anyone's feelings. The message you want your life to stand for and support is never going to make everyone happy and will hurt someone at some point. Are you going to put the fear of hurting someone before your dreams and your soul's purpose to have your voice heard? Any of this relate to you?

Pick one of the shadows that hit your gut or heart in an emotionally triggering way and start the work to clean up the dark side of the feminine. **The individual work you do helps all of us. Then ask yourself this question:** Is there any part of you or any part of your history where you have *been* this quality? Breathe into the energy of compassion as you realize you have that quality within you, just like everyone else. If it's made conscious it is your ally. If it remains unconscious it can be your downfall.

CHAPTER FIFTEEN SUMMARY

You are all aspects of humanity and they all serve a purpose.

Our dark shadows do not usually get our attention in a healthy and productive way.

Women are not perfect and men are not the enemy.

You are a victim *and* a perpetrator

The energies of competitive, authority, needy and selfish are helpful at times.

CHAPTER SIXTEEN

THE "C" WORD: GAIN CONTROL BY GIVING IT UP

One of the deepest habitual patterns that we have
is the feeling that
the present moment is not good enough.

~Pema Chodron

We have now come to what could be the most life-changing chapter of this book for you. I have not broached this subject earlier because many of us, consciously or unconsciously, do not want to hear it. Most people will react to this chapter in one of the following three ways:

1. Their ego will make them think, "*I am not ready for this,*" or "*I don't understand this,*" and they will flick through the chapter without realizing much of its power, OR
2. They will say, "*Yes, I know this already. I've heard it all before, I've already done so much self-growth,*" and they will flick through the chapter without going to the next level of awareness, OR
3. They will notice their resistance or complacency, but at the same time will be open and introspective and eager to go deeper with this spiritual practice. I invite you to join this last group as we explore the topic of controlling one's life.

There is a beautiful paradox in life, which is when we give up control, we gain more freedom, power, and relaxation on our path towards true happiness than we ever thought possible. Most people are on a constant cycle of wanting more money, more "stuff," more clients, more praise, or more love, all in order to feel fulfilled. In order to truly experience all life has to offer, we have to be willing to give up control and stop pretending we know how the entire universe works. There is so much outside pressure associated with being "in control," but we do not have to take it on. Instead, we need to make a big leap and dive into the mystery of what is going on around us. We are invited to let go of the need to control everything and live instead with questions like, "What is really going on here?" and "What is moving my body right now?" and "Who am I?" These questions will humbly remind us that we don't have it all figured out—and we don't need to.

One of the biggest life lessons for a powerful *and* feminine woman is trust—trust in herself, trust in a partner, trust in life. If a woman isn't able to trust, she can very easily become controlling, lose power, hurt relationships, and be perceived as overly masculine. She may attempt to manage the people and events in her life in order to feel somewhat in control. This may look like an attempt to make a love relationship work when it really doesn't, or forcing motivation into a project she isn't passionate about, or trying to manage others' reactions to her, or repressing her emotions so she always appears upbeat. Trying to maintain control of our lives can be done in subtle and obvious ways, but is often counterproductive and moves us out of the "flow."

Letting go of control doesn't mean that you won't do anything or that you won't get anywhere; in fact, you will probably do more and get further once you have been able to let go. That has been my experience. Whenever I let go of attempting to control my life, it's like releasing the handbrake in my car. I receive more intuitive guidance that propels me forward to meet the right person, or to come up with a profitable business idea, or to create a solution for a current challenge I am facing. Always! It's amazing! When you let go, there is more forward motion, with less energy used to get you to where you want to go—as long as you are taking action on that internal guidance you receive.

Letting go of control can be both scary and exhilarating. It's like being on a trapeze, ready to swing. Just before you are about to release your grip, you know there will be a moment after you let go when you cannot see the other person there to catch you—you'll be flying, with no idea whether you'll fall and injure yourself or be caught. I myself have had a love-hate relationship with my own practice of letting go, but trust comes when we realize that there is a Grand Power there to catch us. You might call it God, Source, or Universal Love, but your divine partner is always there, ready to do so much more than just catch you—it will help you soar, again and again. It will help you take flight, but you need to first leap. Are you willing to let go?

TRUST THE NATURE OF TIMING

It was love at first sight when I first visited Ashland, Oregon, on holiday from Australia. It was early January, and every building in the historic downtown was still aglow with fairy lights that had not yet been turned off from Christmas. The sight of real snow on the majestic mountain tops was a first for this girl from the "Sunburned Country." That trip proved to be one of the most life-changing experiences of my life. I not only fell in love with the town but was also offered an exciting job opportunity—which meant sponsorship into the country I had dreamed of living in.

And, to top it all off, I met the man of my dreams. . .

Robert was the first man I had dated who was also on a personal and spiritual growth path like my own. I was captured by his deep-set blue eyes and chiseled cheek bones that could have put him on the cover of any men's magazine. He was beautiful, inside and out. In an instant, we felt an intense connection. I could feel it was my destiny to live in Ashland, and Robert was what I called "God's bait," that extra incentive that would get me back no matter what obstacles I might face. This was my first real shot at true love.

When I returned to Australia from that visit, I tried to speed the process up so I could get back to Ashland as soon as possible. I felt aggravated when things moved slower than I wanted. I didn't want to lose the connection I had with Robert by being absent for too long. I did all that was in my control to make sure I wouldn't return one day later than necessary. Even so, four impatient months passed in Australia before I finally got everything approved by immigration to come back to the States and work legally. I was due to arrive in Ashland on May 7 but had to change my flight for a week later due to a last-minute hold-up at the consulate's office. I ended up arriving back in town on May 15. As I started to see the Siskiyou Mountains draw near, my stomach filled with racing energy of both nerves and excitement.

I called Robert within hours of arriving. That night, after an hour in front of the mirror and a glass of wine to calm my nerves, he picked me up for dinner. To my disappointment, I didn't experience the same comfort with him that I had remembered. After making some small talk, the conversation eventually became serious. Robert stared at me across the table with apologetic eyes and told me that he had just met someone—five days earlier! He was going to pursue a relationship with her. He said, "Given the timing of it all, I thought this was 'a sign.' I really feel a strong connection with her." Oh yeah, and to add insult to injury . . . her name was also Rachael. My heart felt like it had been ripped out of my chest and thrown into my curry to burn. I was devastated and embarrassed. The only option I had was to finish my dinner and pretend as best I could that I was okay with the news. I wanted to blame the timing of everything. I was supposed to have been here with him seven days earlier—if I had just arrived here when I should have, everything would have been different.

Six months later, I saw Robert again. He looked dull and stressed. Rachael was pregnant, and he admitted that he was very unhappy with the relationship but saw no way out. I have to admit, hearing his news helped with my heart's rehabilitation. I could see how lucky I was not to be the "Rachael" in this mess.

Robert and I did stay in contact on and off, and through the occasional meetings I could see how he would not have been a good match for me—at all! And, of course, as a result of all this I was free to eventually meet Datta, who couldn't have been more perfectly hand-picked for me (and I for him). Through this experience, I became more attuned to the importance and incomprehensible nature of timing—and that trying to control it can be futile and not always in our best interest.

Is there anything you are feeling impatient about? Are you open to trusting the timing of things a little more? Your patience could be as important as who you spend the rest of your life with.

TRUST THE DIRECTION OF YOUR LIFE

I believe we all have a "divine purpose" or "soul's calling." Some have tapped into it and keep listening to it for more guidance, thereby flowing towards more and more inner happiness and outer success; others haven't quite discerned what it is but know there is a strong impulse for something greater to be expressed through them, and they want to know what it is. One of the main reasons people get stuck in trying to live their purpose is that they try to control the specific details of what it must look like. Your purpose has much less to do with what business or project you are going to start and much more to do with who you are to *Be* in this world—and for this world.

If you want to trust the direction of your life, clear your slate of any ideas you have for it. Be open to anything, and from that place of letting go, ask for guidance. Don't expect it to come from a booming voice in the sky, but ask. Meditate on the question, "*What is my highest calling for this life?*" Notice and follow what happens.

I have often tried to control what my soul's purpose should be, or what direction I think it should go in. At times, I've been stuck in fearful strategic thinking about how to make money, what type of seminars have the widest market, and what strategy makes the best business sense, instead of listening to that sometimes quiet, sometimes undeniable voice inside me that knows the way to a successful and fulfilling career.

A mentor of mine, Gary Ferguson, once said, "When it comes to following your soul's calling, Rachael Jayne, it's like you are sitting on the river bank. You are close, but you are not in the river. Once you let go of the safety of the banks and jump into the river, you will be in the flow, and there will be no stopping you." Years after Gary had said this to me, I still found myself wanting to cling to those banks as a way of remaining in control of my life. The irony is that when I finally did give up that control, I was offered all the guidance I needed, and everything started to change.

I began to harness the power of this guidance, and life became more inspired. I started experimenting with questions I wanted answers to, questions I had never asked before. One question I asked was, *Is there anything I need to do to connect with the love of my life?* When I asked this, I put myself into a loving and grateful space, expecting to be supported but not attached to any answer. I closed my eyes and was stunned to see the word *SING!* starting to appear in the black space behind my eyelids. The letters were in neon lights, with fireworks going off all around them. I was at first resistant to this information, as I had been in the entertainment business for many years and had no interest in re-entering that industry. I was burned out and couldn't see it happening again. Six months later, however, after a series of serendipitous events and realizations, I did, indeed, decide to start singing again. I asked my friend, Datta, whom I had known for a couple of years, to help me form a band, as he was an excellent bass player and knew many of the musicians in town. To make a long story short, I started singing, and in the process I fell in love with my bass player and dear friend—who is now my husband and the love of my life. The moral of the story? When you ask for guidance and stop controlling the way it comes and on what schedule it should arrive, magic happens.

One common challenge I see with most of my clients is the willingness to give up the notion that they are in complete control of their life. Whether the issue they are struggling with is about finding the perfect job, meeting the love of their life, or simply solving a problem, they think the responsibility of coming up with the solution or the next step lies with them alone. They over-analyze everything with "why" questions—Why does this always happen? Why did I create this? Why have I not released this pattern yet?

No more "why" questions that you think you have to figure out! Please! This keeps you in a seeking mode and not in the present moment. You don't need to know why. You don't need to be in control. You have a divine partner in all of this, whether you see that as God, Guides, Spirit, or the Universe. Your role in this divine partnership is to be the visionary. You are the one who needs to get clear on your heart's true desires and then follow through with action steps when you receive guidance. Your divine partner's role is to figure out the "how." If you've read a lot of self-help books, this may sound trite, but it's true. Your divine partner can see the bigger picture. This higher power can see where everything links up in this "matrix of life." You are not in this alone: Remember that you have access to spiritual guidance always.

EXERCISE #26

What is a challenge or decision point that you are facing right now that you would like some guidance on? Write that down in your journal to refer to in a few minutes.

Be still for 3-5 minutes and deliberately make yourself feel as peaceful and as emotionally uplifted as you possibly can. You may picture in your mind someone you love and the things you are most grateful for, in order to reach a joyful state.

Feel grounded in your womb space, and affirm that you are unattached to receiving the answer you want, or any answer, for that matter. Being unattached to getting an answer helps to stay in a peaceful and joyful state. When you feel you have let go of control, ask about the challenge you want some guidance on.

Be open to an answer coming in any form—a word, a visual picture, or a feeling, etc. Give it time, and stay unattached. Have your journal ready to write down anything that comes. Do not judge the way the guidance comes to you, be grateful for it. Do not judge the information you receive while you are receiving it, just write it down.

It is important to stay grateful for this partnership with your divine power, and say, "Thank you for this guidance." If you do not believe you can access this guidance, you will create a self-fulfilling prophecy; be patient, and stay grateful for the guidance that you do get.

(There is a guided meditation on my Feminine Presence Meditations CD that will help you create the optimal state to ask these questions. To find out more, visit, **www.FeminineMeditations.com**)

CONTROLLING OTHERS

When you feel the need to control somebody else, you lose energy and personal power. In the past, I would often try to control my relationships with men in subtle ways. If I met a guy who I was attracted to, I would put a lot of thought energy into trying to get him to call me, or trying to orchestrate a way that we could meet again, rather than letting go of any need to control the situation and trusting that if it was meant to be he would call. I could feel myself losing my power through all of this effort—some nights, the discomfort in my heart would overwhelm me. It did, indeed, feel like I was giving away my personal power.

I see a lot of people in business, too, trying to control others, and it is a big turn-off. We all know the feeling of being "grasped at" for business, as if someone's self-esteem depends on our saying "yes." It's both sad and uncomfortable. When we get too attached to anyone being a client or customer, we lose our personal power and the magnetic presence we have that draws people into our business in the first place.

It's been such a relief to know that I don't need to continue to "sell" people on my programs and classes. All I need to do is educate and share with love and enthusiasm why this work will change someone's life—they decide whether they want to do it or not. I love to learn about marketing and do what it takes to promote my work, but it's always from a place of trust that the perfect ladies will find me and the *Art of Feminine Presence* work.

There is a shift that happens when you move from feeling like you have to control the sale to trusting in perfection and timing. I felt that shift happen this week. There is a woman who has been considering doing my teacher training for the *Art of Feminine Presence*. This woman is spiritually grounded, connected to her physical and energetic body, and a facilitator and teacher in her own right. She is perfect for it! For a moment, I moved into the place of really wanting her to be part of the next training and feeling an attachment to that. It felt horrible. It did not relax me; instead, it made me feel like I could "lose out" on something if she said no. I could feel my energy leaking out of me.

I caught myself in the act of trying to be in control, released my attachment, and moved into a state of trust, and immediately I felt great again. Your body is a great meter for when you are losing energy from trying to control someone or something: When you control, you feel bad, and when you trust, you feel good. It's that simple.

Some of the most common complaints men have about women are related to feeling controlled by us. One of the biggest gifts a woman can give a man is freedom. Don't try to control him, finish his sentences, or criticize the way he does something—this reduces his masculine strength and pushes him away. Let him fly away whenever he wants to—if he doesn't come back, he was never yours to begin with. I remind myself of this all the time in order to feed my marriage. I encourage Datta to hang out with "the boys" as often as he likes. He is a dancer and a strong lead, so when he goes out dancing, women line up for him. If he feels like dancing one night and I don't, I say, "Go on, dear, make the girls happy." We have a laugh, but I truly mean it. I trust him, and I show him that, and he always comes back even more appreciative and committed to me.

I see many women who try to control their men. It's hard to watch. They tell them they don't want them spending time with other women friends, they get angry and demanding when they don't get their own way, and they get jealous easily. If you see yourself in some of this description, do whatever inner work you need to in order to move past the fear that is arising in your relationships. This fear usually points to abandonment issues. Do things that will build your self-esteem, your self-worth, both while you are single and in relationship. If you don't, this will become a constant theme for you, and you'll push many great relationships away.

EXERCISE #27

Look at your behaviors with partners, lovers, customers, and possible clients, and ask yourself this journal question: What are the ways that you overtly or subtly try to control others?

LETTING GO OF CONTROL INCREASES YOUR MAGNETIC PRESENCE

When you hold on tight to something you don't want to let go of, you have to clench your fist, constrict your energy, and not move your hand. When you let go of your hold, your physical hand and the energy inside it are freed up to move again.

Your personal presence increases when your body and energy are moving in spontaneous and authentically expressive ways. This is why great actors, dancers, and singers have a lot of personal magnetism: They have practiced lots of different ways to move and how not to get stuck in any one particular role they think they should be in. It's why men who can dance with free-flowing movement in their neck, torso, and arms are more attractive to women: When there is more movement inside their bodies, they are perceived to have more strength and vitality. It's why so many professional photo shoots have a fan blowing and the subject moving: It creates a sense of movement, which creates more personal presence. And it's why overly posed photos may show someone's physical beauty but not do justice to their personal presence.

When someone doesn't feel safe to "let go," it often shows up in their body. No matter what shape or size they are, people who try to be in control of their life are less expressive and tend to have stagnant energy. When someone is more present to the moment and allows themselves to move any way they want, their energy feels more alive.

EXERCISE #28

As you continue to read, take some deep, easy breaths and bring your attention inside your body. Notice where there is flow and where there may be constriction or a block. Start with your feet and lower legs. Then, move your attention up to your upper legs, hips and pelvis. Notice where there is spaciousness and flow and where there is not. Slowly move your attention to your torso. Feel your belly, your heart, and your back. Where is there flow, and where is there constriction? Finally, check in with your neck, arms, and face. Is there spaciousness and flow there, or not?

Bring your attention now to the part of your body that feels the least amount of flow and the least amount of easy movement. Breathe into that place in your body as you feel it softening. Send loving attention to it as you move it gently, imagining more flow in this area of your body. Remember, movement and flow increase your magnetic presence.

Find a practice that helps you unlock your body so you can move through your day more freely. Take up a dance class, an acting improvisation class, or a form of exercise that isn't too structured. Create spaciousness and flow in your body, and this, in turn, will create spaciousness and flow in your mind. In my *Art of Feminine Presence* intensives, the subtle movement meditation called the "Feminine Presence Meditation" I teach is an integral practice that moves feminine energy through the body, increases a woman's personal presence, and helps her to let go and receive to a greater degree in all areas of her life.

BECOMING FULLY WOMAN

One of the most inspiring success stories I know of from *Art of Feminine Presence* comes from Monica's journey. She showed up to her first training as a man in woman's clothing. She would cover more of her face than necessary with a wig that was stiffer than her personality. She looked down a lot, her walk was stilted, but she had a wicked—and hilarious—self-deprecating sense of humor. She was the first transgendered woman to join us for a training and we all fell in love with her instantly. Her courage and authenticity were extremely attractive.

The first phase of her transformation was to sense the feminine essence that could fuel her body to run more feminine energy than masculine. When she dropped into the feminine presence meditations and let that energy take over her body, it was so stunning in made many of us tear up.

The second phase of the transformation was to relax into receiving affectionate attention from her "sisters." We all need candid feedback, loving eyes, accepting hugs. As she received this in the dosage she was comfortable with, the ease of her voice and gestures became more feminine without her usual effort to make them sound and look feminine. Her energetic presence was becoming a woman.

The third phase of her transformation was to work through the layers of fear that arose as she got clear she wanted to live full-time as a woman. She shared with me many times previously that she would never do so, as she had only been doing that privately at home and within the transgendered community overseas. With a very successful career in finance and investing and knowing full well the gross mis-treatment many transgendered people are subjected to, she felt there was a lot to lose. As her presence grew, her sense of safety grew, and in turn her authentic desires grew. Even though Monica lived in a town that was not obviously one of the most progressive in the world, she finally announced her true nature and started living life exactly how she wanted.

The fourth phase of her transformation came when we did a powerful process with her 'light shadow.' The quality she felt she couldn't own was 'inspirational.' Everyone knew she was inspirational, and bathed in it whenever we were around her, but it hadn't 'dropped in' for her, so the brakes were on in regard to her soul's purpose. She eventually took the time to own it, through every cell of her body. As she kept revealing her true feminine heart, it was impossible for anyone not to be inspired. She was voted in as President of her town's Rotary club, was featured in the local paper and other forms of media, and eventually wrote a book *Me: The Gift of Being Transgendered.* When the odds are stacked against you, the inspirational mark you leave is usually far greater than you can imagine.

RACHAEL JAYNE GROOVER

THE ART OF FOLLOWING

There are more and more times these days when it feels like something or someone greater is moving me to do or say something. I get this sense when I am in the flow with my writing, when I'm teaching, or when I'm offering a friend words of wisdom. It feels like I am just a vessel for some greater energy and wisdom. Being aware of this allows me to relax and let the "flow" happen.

Learning how to follow a higher guidance or another person is an art form the feminine essence woman naturally becomes skilled at. This type of following is not blind faith, just empowered listening. It's about being sensitive enough to follow your inner impulse to move rather than the habitual way you move. It's about trusting a higher power or another person who is worthy of your trust so you can enjoy the feeling of "letting go" and being taken for a ride.

It feels pleasurable to follow. Think of dancing with a strong masculine man who knows how to dance and lead well. It doesn't get much better than that for me. When I can relax as the follower, I don't have to work out which direction to go, what steps to take, or who I may bump into; but instead I can focus on expressing myself, connecting with him, and being totally in my body. Many Western women resist the art of following because we have not had many positive examples of following. Instead, we have seen the opposite, where following has equaled giving our power away or, in more dire circumstances, has allowed people to get away with brutal domination. This is not the type of following I am talking about. The type of following I'm talking about can only happen when you choose a partner, a friend, a leader, and/or a higher power that you can put your trust in. They must prove themselves. I wouldn't continue dancing with a man who kept bumping me into others on the dance floor. I wouldn't follow a man anywhere unless he had proven his trustworthiness and loyalty. You can't let go until you trust. Following without trust is insane; not following because you think it's weak is just as foolish.

How can you become more sensitive to the impulse that wants to move you? How can you follow that impulse? Next time you are having a conversation with someone, try feeling what wants to be said through you instead of cramming the space with too many words. Next time you walk into a room, try following the impulse that says, "Go to that side of the room" rather than the other. Next time you have to choose someone to work with, try checking in with what the impulse inside you is saying. What choice wants to be made through you?

EXERCISE #29

Put on some of your favorite instrumental music and give up the need to move to it in a certain way. Keep your eyes closed. Breathe deeply into your belly for a minute or so, and wait until you feel "moved" to move. When you feel an impulse to move— in your hand or arm or hip—let it move you. Take it slowly to begin with, and stay aware of any habitual moves that you would ordinarily do on the dance floor. Resist these habits. This practice is about being moved physically by something greater than you, rather than by the way your mind thinks you should move. Oh yeah, and you are allowed to enjoy it ☺.

Developing a close relationship with my divine partner is the primary way I have developed a greater sense of trust in myself, others, and life. I choose those beliefs that feel good to me and help me have the deepest trust in life. When I trust, I let go of trying to control everything. I smile more, and I have more physical energy and more bounce in my step. I am happier. I have less drama filling up my head, and I can hear the voice of inspiration clearer. If you find yourself at a time in your life where you want to let go of the trapeze you've been clinging to, trust has to be present in order for you to make the leap. You have to let go of one side before you can be caught on the other. The whole time you are in the air, not able to see who is there to catch you, you have to trust. Your divine partner is like your trapeze partner that you cannot see. Your life will only take flight when you start to trust that greater power and let go of the control you only think you have.

CHAPTER SIXTEEN SUMMARY

If you don't "let go" and trust both yourself and life, you are likely to become controlling, lose power and relationships, and be perceived as overly masculine.

Trust in the perfect timing of events. You do not always know what is in your highest good or in the highest good of others.

One of the biggest complaints men have about women is that they can be too smothering and clingy. Let your man fly away, and see if he comes back.

Letting go of control increases your magnetic presence. When you let go, you create more flow and movement in your body. This, in turn, allows for more authentic self expression and spontaneity. Stay aware of where there is flow in your body and where there is constriction.

Be a vessel for the divine wisdom and power that wants to move through you. Follow the subtle impulses to move in a certain direction, to contact a certain person, or to share a piece of wisdom.

CHAPTER SEVENTEEN

THE POWER OF SURRENDER

Friends, the Beloved is a lion,
We are a deer that has a bad leg and can't run.
Cornered, with no way to escape, in those arms,
the most we can do is give up.

~Rumi

If you are committed to your personal growth and being aligned with your divine purpose, at some point you will experience what I call a "spiritual crisis." This may show up as a series of small challenges, or it may be a cataclysmic event that makes you feel like a train just hit you. This "crisis" will call you to give up your limited idea of who you think you are and devote your life to something much larger than yourself. It is in this devotion and absolute surrender to something larger that the feminine essence finds its most powerful form of expression. Until you gain the humility and courage to surrender, you will always feel like you are living on the river banks of life—and never in the powerful flow of the river.

The year 2006 felt like a breakthrough year for me. My confidence and clarity in my mission were expanding, and my tolerance for "staying small" was evaporating. It was the year I stepped out of my comfort zone, started my own side business, and began to teach my own message. I was making more money than I'd ever made before in my job, and I was happy. It was also the year I fell deeply in love—the man of my dreams finally came knocking on my door, supporting me in more ways than I could have imagined. Life had become brilliantly colorful. And then everything changed.

During August of that year, while on a business trip to England, I started to notice my lower back muscles vying for my attention. Twinges of pain came and went, and it started to become more and more uncomfortable to walk around in my "sensible" 3-inch heels. One week into my trip, I awoke in the middle of the night in excruciating pain. I could not move—if I did, even an inch, pain would surge up and down my body, bringing me close to losing consciousness. I instinctively knew I had to get myself onto a hard surface, so I dragged myself off the low mattress I was on and pulled myself over the carpet onto the cold, hardwood floor, like an injured snake. I was foolishly too polite to awaken my new friend, Sarah, who was hosting me in London, so there I lay, on the opposite side of the world from home, frightened, in pain, and trying not to cry so as not to move my body into an acute spasm again. The anticipation of an ice-pack and painkillers kept me going until Sarah finally found me early the next morning face down on her living room floor. It would be two months before I would be able to fly home in a first-class, 6-foot bed.

Eighteen months after that painful adventure, the picture still hadn't changed much. If you had observed me then, you would have seen me lying on my stomach in bed, writing as best I could, waiting for the next painkiller to kick in. Between the occasional spurts of inspiration, you would also have seen a lot of tears and heard many shrieks, and on one occasion you would have heard the sound of my frail body crashing to the shower floor, passed out from the pain. I was in a constant state of sleep deprivation, as I couldn't get more than two hours sleep at a time, and I was on the verge of depression.

My chiropractor told me in the beginning that it may take up to a year or two to fully recover. The unanimous position amongst all my healers was to avoid surgery, at least for as long as possible, and so I took advantage of as many alternative and traditional treatments as I could. These offered some relief, followed by more pain, followed by more relief, and then more pain. Just as the hope of sustained healing would start looking inevitable, BAM!—down I would go again. There were days when I wanted someone to pick up a gun and put me out of my misery. I was not getting any answers to what I considered to be the key questions to my full recovery: What was the underlying cause of this injury? How could I use all my physical and metaphysical knowledge and wisdom to heal myself? Why would this happen at what was otherwise the happiest time of my life?

I was not handling my situation well. I did not want to concede that this might remain my predicament for a long time to come, but I felt trapped. I felt like a victim. This situation was *not okay* with me. I wanted the pain to STOP!

WHAT YOU RESIST PERSISTS

Whatever you give your attention to grows. The thoughts you have, when coupled with emotional intensity, become the reality in your life. This is why positive thinking helps you manifest what you most want. And it's also why some situations you *don't* want to happen keep happening—in spite of your positive thinking.

Have you ever heard the saying, "What you resist persists?" Another way of saying this is that what you don't want often sticks around because you give it attention, focus, and emotional intensity—even when you don't mean to. Imagine picking up something you don't want, holding it in your fisted hand, then pushing it aside with one arm, and holding it there so it doesn't spring back at you—and then saying, "I am now not going to give this thing any attention." You are fooling yourself! You can look the other way, but you are still using all the might in your arm to keep that dark thing you don't want to face in place. And this is exactly what happens when you resist something that is happening in your life—all your energy flows in the direction you don't want.

Positive thinking alone will not change your resistance to something. Have you ever been confused about why a situation you don't want keeps "sticking to you," even when you are putting a lot of energy into "positive thinking?" That's because for positive thinking to be effective, it *must* be accompanied by emotional intensity—or energy. When you *don't* want something, you may not realize the amount of negative focus, or energy, you are sending towards the very thing you don't want. Positive thinking has a great effect on your life—

keep doing it! But always notice where you are sending your energy what you are most resistant to, and what you are most scared of or in judgment about.

PRACTICAL STEPS TO LETTING GO OF RESISTANCE

There are four primary steps to letting go of resistance:

1. Become aware of what you are resisting.
2. Feel the resistance—breathe into it, meet it with compassion and forgiveness, but don't wallow in it.
3. Use the power of prayer and contemplation to ask the question, "Would I be okay if nothing ever changed?" and
4. When the resistance and worry come again, which they will, meet them with the words, "It's okay, I hear you, but I am not scared of you anymore."

On my 237th visit to the chiropractor (that is a literal number, by the way), I lay on the adjusting table and looked up at compassionate, wise, and intelligent Dr. Welch. It was one of those dark days following yet another agonizing setback. He stopped his treatment and looked at me with kind eyes, and in a **soft voice he said, "It may be time to consider surgery."**

Tears welled up in me, and my head started to shake. *No, no, what are you saying?* I said to myself. All sorts of fearful thoughts took over. *I don't have health insurance in this country.* ***If I have surgery, I'll have to fly all the way back to Australia*** *for the procedure and be away from Datta and my closest friends for quite some time.* ***I can't afford to take another year to recover from something like that.*** Dr. Welch took my hand and said, "Just sit with the possibility. If it's a way to give you your life back, it's worth considering." We talked well into his next appointment as he helped me see that even though I knew the truth of the saying, "What you resist persists," I was caught in the throes of major opposition to my situation.

For the next week, I spent many hours in prayer and contemplation, asking myself, *Would I be okay if I were in chronic pain for the rest of my life? Would I be okay if nothing ever changed?* **I knew I had to find a way to look at my situation** with new eyes if I was going to be able to let go of the fear and resistance that had such a hold on me. I played various scenes of possibilities on the screen of my imagination. I saw how I could use voice-recognition software that would take dictation, which would save me from sitting at my desk too long. I could do more of my speeches and classes in tele-seminar format rather than traveling. And, even though my social life would look different, I imagined holding great parties at home so my friends could come to me.

I prayed for the strength and courage to know that I could face anything life threw at me, and I gave up my mental and emotional struggle with my back. It didn't happen overnight, but within a few days I started to feel my body and heart soften as I heard my own soothing answer: *Yes, I would be okay. If nothing ever changed, I could still live a happy life and do my work in the world. I would find a way.* Within a few weeks, without surgery, I was almost completely pain free, and, as the months have passed, my body has continued to become stronger and stronger.

The process and power of surrender are not easy to explain in words, but experiencing them has had a profound spiritual impact on my life. Since this experience of surrender, I have worried a lot less. There is more ease and relaxation in my life, as I don't push too hard to make things happen anymore. I still do what I need to do, but instead of judging that it has to happen a certain way and on a certain timeline, I have the patience to wait for the right moment. My close relationships, too, are more harmonious, as I live more of my days with flexibility and trust.

EXERCISE #30

What are you most scared of or in judgment about these days? What is it that keeps you up at night or activates negative feelings within you? Is it the state of your health, your financial situation, your being single? You may be resisting how someone else is being or not being. Note some of your thoughts about this resistance in your journal.

Set some time aside in the next few days to really feel your resistance. Acknowledge it. Let it be present.

It's common to think of forgiveness in terms of forgiving yourself or another person, or even an event that has occurred. But you can also forgive your emotions. When you bring forgiveness to an emotion that is present, the resistance stops and the emotion often passes by effortlessly. I have had clients share that they had never thought about forgiving an emotion before. It's a simple concept but one that is hard to remember when you are in the middle of an emotional tail-spin. The first thing most people do when they try to shift an emotion is an attempt to push it aside and focus on something positive. But this creates resistance. When we instead bring the emotion towards us and forgive it, it disappears.

Next time you feel frustrated, or fearful, or sad, instead of trying to make yourself *not* feel these things, feel the forgiveness in your heart and belly for whatever emotion you're feeling. See how beautiful it is, and bring it in close. You will be surprised at the freedom you will feel as a result.

EXERCISE #31

As you write about and really feel your resistance, notice that, instead of wallowing in whatever emotion you are feeling, you can meet it with compassion and forgiveness. Forgiveness neutralizes resistance. The moment we forgive anything, it stops holding us back. Practice forgiving the emotions that arise for you. When you feel sadness, say to yourself, "I forgive the sadness that is arising in this moment."

YOU CAN'T MANIPULATE THE UNIVERSE

You can't do any of these steps we've talked about as a way to manipulate God, or the Universe, to get what you want. It doesn't work that way. It's not about pretending to let go of resistance so that a favorable outcome will occur; you must be totally willing to surrender and be okay with your life either changing or never changing. When you can reach that place, you will have truly surrendered all resistance.

After accepting the possibility that I may always have back pain, and being okay with it, I experienced many wonderful months of physical strength and flexibility. I was so grateful the horror was finally over. Or was it?

At 4:30 pm on the afternoon before my wedding ceremony with Datta, I started to feel those painful twinges. By 7:00 pm, they had become full-blown spasms that caused me to bow out of the pre-wedding festivities and head straight to bed with ice-packs, painkillers and a strong dose of anxiety. I couldn't believe the timing!

I woke up the next day feeling somewhat better, but by the time I walked down the aisle I had taken so much Vicodin to numb the pain that I was pretty drugged up. Thankfully, the Vicodin, combined with the awesome experience of marrying the man of my dreams kept me "high" enough that day that I was able to make it through and be genuinely happy. It was truly a magical day, a fairytale wedding in the stunning garden setting of Lithia Park in Ashland, Oregon, but by noon the following day I could not walk.

For the next two weeks, I could not walk or even stand up on my own. I was in just as much pain as I had been in while in England, and instead of spending quality time with my family (who had traveled all the way from Australia) and preparing for our honeymoon, I was doing anything and everything I could think of to deal with the pain. But the amazing thing was that, even with all the pain I was experiencing, these were some of the happiest weeks I can remember. I really was okay with what was happening because I wasn't resisting it. I thought, *Okay, here I am. My body is "freaked out" about something, and it's time to enjoy the "down time" as much as I can.* I knew the power of surrender, and so I just stayed with it. If I had tried to manipulate the Universe months before, when I had first faced my resistance to the pain, I would have reacted now with anger, or frustration, or hopelessness—wondering why "the steps" weren't working. But for the second time, I was okay with the prospect that I might experience these intense pain periods forever, and that if that was what God had in store for me I would deal with it. And, like the tides, the pain came in, and then the pain went out. I was grateful that this pain period was shorter than any other.

Have you ever been confused or frustrated and said, "I thought I had cleared that?" or "I thought I was over that?"—with the expectation that healing a physical or emotional wound was a onetime deal? Life is dynamic and ever changing. *You* are dynamic and ever changing. Having your buttons pushed by someone in this moment, or having some pain show up in your body after years of good health, doesn't mean you didn't work on that issue earlier in your life. The present moment always offers something new. Instead of being caught in a cycle of over-analyzing or beating yourself up, come into the present moment and ask,

"How can I come back into alignment with the power of who I really am, right now, and surrender any resistance to what is happening?"

The word "surrender" can hold negative associations for some people. But surrendering is not about giving in or claiming to be a victim to something outside of yourself; to surrender, in spiritual and psychological terms, means to give up your individual will and your thoughts, ideas, and deeds to the will of a divine power or higher power. Remember, you have a partnership with a higher power; you don't have to work every detail of your life out by yourself. When you have a problem that you don't know the solution to, give it over to this higher power. Whenever I get stuck in doubt, wondering how on earth I am going to make something happen, I remember I don't need to know *how* it's going to happen, I just need to stay clear on my intention and ask for guidance. My Higher Power always knows the most beneficial way to accomplish things, and it's always much better than anything I could have drummed up anyway.

EXERCISE #32

Write and say an affirmation or incantation every day that will remind you to surrender and partner with your higher power. For example, my affirmation is, "Guide me, protect me, I will follow through. Thank you for the guidance you give, I'm open to receiving more and more." I say this in the morning as I exercise or meditate.

The way I sense our collective consciousness in the West right now, we are like a flock of wounded birds. As a society, we are not moving forward with vibrancy or full range of movement. Many people are struggling, just trying to hold on through this unstable economic, political, environmental, and social time until things improve. But the problem is that this volatility is most likely not going to pass quickly; it is most likely going to become a way of life for a long time, not something that we just "get through." So how are we going to *be* if nothing changes, and especially if it gets worse?

Part of me would love to be able to tell you with conviction and integrity that everything is going to be alright, that you just have to ignore everyone's negative thinking and read positive self-help books every day. But the truth is that even though at the highest level we will ultimately be alright, I don't know if everything is going to work out without massive upheaval and pain. Just like Dr. Welch said to me, "You may have to look at the inevitable."

You may not be sitting here next year with your job or business or health intact. You may be seeing some of the toughest times you've ever had. I don't know what your future brings, but I do know this: Whatever you resist gets harder. Whatever you worry about sticks to you. And if you surrender, with courage and arms wide open, you will experience the magnitude of who you are and a true spiritual liberation. That is a power that no one and nothing—not even a "down" economy —can take away from you.

CHAPTER SEVENTEEN SUMMARY

What you resist persists. Personal power and spiritual liberation come when you surrender to what is happening in the moment.

Surrendering is not about giving in or claiming to be a victim of something outside yourself. In spiritual and psychological terms, surrendering means giving up your individual will, thoughts, ideas, and deeds to the will of a divine, or higher power.

There are four primary steps to letting go of resistance:

1. Become aware of what you are resisting.
2. Feel the resistance. Breathe into it, meet it with compassion and forgiveness, but don't wallow in it.
3. Use the power of prayer and contemplation to ask the question: "Would I be ok if nothing ever changed?"
4. When the resistance and worry come again, which they will, meet them with the words, "It's okay, I hear you, but I am not scared of you anymore."

"Our pain, as uncomfortable as it can be, always offers us a chance to heal more than just our physical bodies."

~Rachael Jayne Groover

CHAPTER EIGHTEEN

MAKING LOVE WITH EVERYTHING

The most beautiful things in the world cannot be seen or even touched, they must be felt with the heart.

~Helen Keller

Throughout this book, we have focused mostly on our "inner work." After all, going within to understand ourselves and our soul's essence is our most important mission as human beings. That said, however, as we cross into new realms of our power *and* femininity, we need to become acutely aware of how we interact with the world around us. The feminine energy is the energy of unity, collaboration, and connection with all. The feminine cares about the collective experience, not just her own, and wants to be present for her whole community in a way that fulfills her. For a feminine essence woman, life is not about sitting on the mountaintop and meditating her way to enlightenment without "getting down and dirty" with the real world. Instead, it's about being "at home" in her womb space and heart, not only when alone but also when others need her or confront her, when she is considering her outer mission in the world, and when she has decisions to make that affect those around her.

Your ability to live in harmony with the rest of the planet, *and* to affect it with your positive mark of feminine power, all boils down to how present you are. There are three main areas you need to be present with in order to be the powerful *and* feminine woman you want to be. Those are being present with your mission in the world, being present with your decisions, and being present in conversation and conflict.

BE PRESENT WITH YOUR MISSION IN THE WORLD

Most people ask themselves, "What have I come here to do?" They struggle to find their "life's purpose," as if there was only one right answer. But the question that will most help you live your purpose is not "What have I come here to do?" but rather "Who have I come here to *be*?" It's who you are and what you are demonstrating through your actions that matter most, not whether you are an acupuncturist, a lawyer, or a candle maker. If you currently struggle with the question, "What is my purpose?", don't be too consumed with thoughts about what to do; instead, focus on who you want to *be* in this next phase of your life. How do you want to express yourself through your *Being* and *Presence*? I invite you to write down the five to seven key qualities you want to *be* that feel central to why you are here on the planet. For example, some of my words—the qualities I want to be—are Compassionate, Healthy, Spiritually Aware, Confident, Joyful, and Authentic.

Whether I'm singing, leading a class, organizing a social event with a friend, or writing, I'm clear that my mission in the world is to demonstrate these qualities. Once you consistently embody the qualities you choose, then be open to receiving more clarity on what it is you want to do.

One of the most helpful ways I became clear on what I wanted to do as part of my greater mission in life was by taking myself back in history. I asked, "What were the four or five times when I felt most alive, passionate, and happy doing something?" I let the memories bubble up to the surface without trying too hard to reach for them. I remembered one of my favorite music performances in a beautiful auditorium; I remembered a seminar that I was co-leading; I remembered being in a group doing deep spiritual work and being supported in that. What scenes come to mind when you recall those times where you felt so "juiced" by what you were doing? What do these things all have in common?

You might find that the scenes from your memory don't have much in common with each other, but don't worry about that. Stay open and curious about how these things may come together to be part of your larger mission in the world. I love to do a range of things, but for a long time I struggled with trying to strategically make it all work. I believed I had to choose one thing over the others. Years ago, if someone had said to me, "You will have a career and fulfilling mission that includes speaking about personal and spiritual development, singing to captive audiences, and teaching femininity and personal presence using your love of dance and energy work, all the while incorporating your love for business and marketing," I would have thought they were crazy. I would have hoped it to be true but thought them crazy nonetheless. This is my reality now. I couldn't have orchestrated it better if I had tried. Stay open to how several of your passions can come together to create a powerful mission in the world for you. Your spiritual guidance is at work. Continue to *be* and *do* what makes you feel alive, and don't forget that you don't have to figure it all out yourself.

I believe one's "mission" or "purpose" is more of a "calling." It's not something we need to figure out. A "calling" is a strong inner impulse toward a particular course of action, especially when it is connected to our spiritual guidance and influence. It's already happening in you. You can hear this "calling" any time you decide to be really present and check in with your self and your spiritual guidance. If you are not receiving much insight in this regard, you might just need more time in silence to listen deeply. Ask questions. Be grateful for the answers that come your way. Be patient. You will know it's your "calling" when it has much less to do with getting your ego's needs met and much more to do with how you positively affect everyone around you and the pure joy of giving your gifts.

There comes a time when your life is not just about you anymore. It's about helping all the world's people. You may still work on your own "issues" and challenges, but they feel small in comparison to what you are really here to *be* and *do*. When you realize that you are here for everyone else, it does not come from a place of superiority. It does not come from forgetting yourself and your own needs and wants. It does not feel like you have to somehow "save the world." When this realization occurs, you won't feel fear or be overwhelmed with responsibility. You won't feel the kind of worry that inhibits you from taking optimistic action. If you do feel burdened with worry and/or responsibility that means you are not in the sweet spot of this realization, even though you might think you are. This knowing that your life is not about you feels like a passionate, joyful stirring deep inside to do something that will improve everyone's life because they are your family too.

It's important to do our inner work first so that we can move from righteousness and fear to humility and optimistic action. Don't side-step your own Shadow Work and try to be somewhere you are not. Don't bypass the fact that you might be at a stage in your life where you need to be more self-centered because you have tended to look after everyone else before yourself. Instead, as you continue your spiritual practice and personal growth, become aware of the times you experience these feelings of fear, overwhelm, and superiority. Notice them when they arise, and wrap them in love and forgiveness. You are not here to save the world from itself, you are here to live in joy, love, and right action to support the world in an enormous transformation that is taking place, right now.

Warning! When you live in love with everyone and everything around you, you will feel more pain than before because your heart will be wide open. At the same time, you will feel more love and compassion than ever before. Keep your energetic boundaries strong, with your "light globe" protecting you, and stay home in your own energetic space. This will keep you safe. But inside this protective space, keep your mind, body, and spiritual connection open. I feel more sensitive to other's pain now than I ever have, but it does not shut me down; rather, it keeps me more present to how I can be of service. Keep your "light globe" on, but don't fear your heart's sweet sensitivity.

EXERCISE #33

What are the five to seven Qualities of Being that you want to express as part of your mission for the world? Write them down, and put them somewhere you'll see them often.

Which scenes from your life arise when you think of times that you felt most alive and living your passion? Write down three or four scenes that come to mind. Then, ask yourself, what is the theme that is common to all of them?

BE PRESENT WITH YOUR DECISIONS

Every decision you make has an effect on someone or something else in the world. That effect might be small or wide, positive or negative, but it reminds us we are not islands unto ourselves rather we are part of a larger world family. If you are really serious about being an inspiring example of feminine power and compassion, you must become more conscious of your day-to-day decisions and how they affect everything and everyone else, not in a way that feels burdensome and overwhelming but in a way that encourages you to live in alignment with what you say and who you want to be. When you make decisions that are *not* in alignment with who you want to be, you consciously or unconsciously feel like a bit of a phony. This holds you back because you don't want to be "found out." But when you "walk your talk," it increases your feeling of self-worth and self-esteem. When you make great decisions, you feel better about yourself, and your personal power increases.

To make empowering decisions, we need as a community to engage in broader ethical discussions. Most people decide what is "right" and "wrong" given what's in their best interest or what their parents, religion, or spiritual group have taught them. In either case, they think there are fixed rules for what is "right" and "wrong" (which frequently and conveniently happen to be what is in their best selfish interest) and fail to see how their decisions affect the rest of the world. It's time to question what is best for the whole and take an active role in inspiring others to take a hard, honest look at what we are doing to each other and the planet—starting with ourselves and our own actions. This is not easy because people are resistant to go there. Even many "conscious" people resist really looking at the ethics of their decisions. I see two main reasons for this resistance.

The first reason is due to the trend in personal growth work and spiritual circles to not judge anything and be okay with whatever is happening in the moment. On the one hand, this is a good thing, as it helps us unwind the pattern of always criticizing and judging our thoughts and behaviors, and letting our inner critic run our lives. On the other hand, it lets us off the hook too easily, and we can become complacent in our decisions and how they affect the world, all the while using spiritual language to justify it. I hear phrases like, "there's no such thing as 'right' and 'wrong,'" and "everything happens for a reason," and "no sentient being can really be harmed at their deepest level." On the one hand, these statements are true. On the other hand, it's dangerous when we swing too far the other way and don't judge anything as "good" or "bad," or "right" or "wrong," and stick our head under the sand, not considering how we affect other individuals and the world itself. When we do this, we can make unconscious decisions that have negative consequences. This complacency can halt our individual spiritual progress.

The second reason why there is so much resistance to looking at how our decisions affect everything else is *convenience.* I can relate to this one the most. It was not convenient for me to realize how many products I used that were harmful to the environment. It was not convenient for me to learn that the meat I ate was produced in a way that caused extreme suffering to animals that had the same level of feeling and personality as my dear pets. It was not convenient for me to realize how much I did not know about the other side of the world and what was happening there. For me, ignorance was convenient. After all, I liked the look of leather boots, I liked the way my hair was held in place with my old hairspray with all its toxic, environmentally harmful ingredients, and I liked the taste of chicken. The changes I finally made were not easy. My choice not to eat meat again was the hardest. I was resistant to the idea for many years and I justified it by thinking, *If I just bless my food before eating it, wouldn't that balance out all the suffering that was caused to the dozen or so cows that contributed to this hamburger?* I really had to look at my ignorance and resistance and ask some hard questions. But when I finally did make the change, I felt so much better both physically and energetically because I was now in alignment with my compassionate side, the side that does not want to cause others unnecessary suffering.

Almost all of us make buying choices every day that have some level of negative impact on other people, animals, or the environment. It can be very difficult to get the information we need to make an informed decision. But let's try anyway to make more informed decisions. You'll need to read a little further than what the Food and Drug Administration or the government reports, as their advice is driven by lobbyists with a lot of money backing them up. It's worth the extra trouble. It doesn't have to be overwhelming. Start small. Make a few changes that you can make now, and then later make a few more. When you talk to others about the decisions you feel are more ethical, don't ask for their personal or spiritual opinion; instead, ask yourself how these decisions may affect our world family as a whole. Personal, religious, and spiritual opinions can be very strong, and people can be very attached—and comfortable—with those opinions. Look at any harm you may be causing as objectively as possible. Ethical decisions need our presence now more than ever as we are in the middle of an environmental, economic, political, and social crisis. We *can* make a difference with our decisions. We *can* cause great change.

EXERCISE #34

What is one small change that you can make in your purchasing decisions that will feel more in alignment with the ethical decisions you want to make?

Are you willing to make this change today?

BE PRESENT IN CONVERSATION AND CONFLICT

No matter how much you practice everything else in this book, if you don't have a high level of presence you won't get far and will always wonder why.

As I shared earlier, certain women walk into a room and are noticed by many. They have an air of confidence and a magnetic quality about them that is attractive and seems effortless. The effortless part of this scenario comes from how "tuned in" a woman is to the present moment. Instead of walking into a room thinking about what happened yesterday or what might happen in two hours, she is in the moment and therefore in her essential power. Being present in the moment increases your magnetic personal presence. It draws people to you because who you are *being* is something people hunger for. Many people have never been in a simple conversation with someone who is totally present with them, let alone being in a conflict with someone who could remain totally present rather than biting back. If you have experienced this, you know the profound gift this type of connection offers. Every interaction with another is affected by how present we can be. When we are present in the moment, we are connected to our loving essence. When we are present in the moment, we are not stuck in our judgments, biases, or beliefs about how someone else or the world should be. This inner "presence" is a State of Being that can change or heal anything that comes into your life, including the people around you who just want to be seen, heard, and loved. Presence with others is the number one thing you must cultivate.

There are many ways we can "pop out" of being present when we engage with another, but the underlying theme of all of them is our need for something to be different than it is. It is our "needs" that get in the way of total presence and unconditional love with another. My presence increased tenfold when I learned what "needs" tended to show up in conversation that took me out of being present with someone. I then chose not to put my attention on those "needs" while I was with another person.

The trainer who had the biggest impact on me while training as a life coach was the articulate and wise Paul Clark, Director of *CWG Coaching Services.*

Paul would often share the following metaphor that explains how your "needs" can easily and dramatically decrease your level of presence:

Imagine that you, as a friend, a sister, a coach, or a coworker, are holding up a mirror for the person you are in conversation with. The more present you are, the cleaner that mirror is for them to see who they really are. When they see who they really are, they feel empowered. If you are in your own judgments or biases ("needs"), you do not have a clear mirror. All your "needs" are being projected onto this mirror and therefore onto the other person. This does not feel good to the other person—they don't feel seen, heard, or felt.

We've all been on the receiving end of someone not being present. It does anything but magnetize us to them. When you are able to observe your "needs" and not project them on to someone else, you will feel great to be around.

What are the "needs" that most often take you out of the present moment, thereby decreasing your magnetic presence?

I have included below 10 of the most common "needs" that get in the way of our effortlessly being present and magnetic. As you read these "needs," ask yourself which ones apply to you. We all fall into each of them at some stage, but there will be ones you tend to get lost in more than others.

Need #1: **The Need to Fix the Problem**

This "need" can show up as always giving advice to others or habitually telling people what to do. You are in this "need" when you find it hard to let someone have their own process. As Paul Clark would say, "You don't know how many times someone needs to hit rock bottom before they are going to change for good. Are you going to deprive them of that chance to finally make a change?" When you are in this "need," your mind is ahead of the present moment, and often you are unaware of what the person is really asking for underneath their words. Do you ever see yourself in this picture?

Need #2: **The Need to be of Service and Value**

This is similar to the "need" to fix the problem, although a little different. Some people's underlying motivation is to always be of help to others so they can feel internally valuable. They feel somehow that they are not valuable enough by just being present and not giving anything. When they are not feeling like they are being of great value to the other person, their own joy in the interaction decreases. Do you ever see yourself in this picture?

***Need #3:* The Need to be Liked**

People often get caught up in the "need" to be liked by the person they are talking to. When this "need" is driving them, their attention is on themselves and their own behavior and not with the other person. When they do not feel the other person is pleased with or likes them, their joy in the interaction decreases. Others can typically sense when someone is coming from a "need to be liked" place versus a present and authentic place. Do you ever see yourself in this picture?

***Need #4:* The Need to Not Have Too Much Silence in the Conversation**

Many people are uncomfortable with silence and therefore fill every second with words and try to avoid a pause in the conversation. They may always jump in quickly after the other person has finished speaking, or they may think of what to say next before the other person has finished speaking. Either way, it makes the other person feel like they are not being fully listened to. Do you ever see yourself in this picture?

***Need #5:* The Need to Have the Person Be Somewhere Further Along on Their Path**

When someone feels this "need" arise, they may often give more advice than called for, are unnecessarily worried or in judgment about the other person, or try to push them into something that they perceive will be best for them, whether it is or not. When they are not able to simply be present with another person where they are, their joy in the interaction decreases. Do you ever see yourself in this picture?

***Need #6:* The Need to Look like You are Competent and Know What You are Talking About**

This "need" also has a person place attention more on themselves than the other person. We can all feel when the other person is more concerned with their image than with us. Do you ever see yourself in this picture?

***Need #7:* The Need to Not Have the Other Person Feel Bad or Uncomfortable**

The present moment may inspire you to call the other person on their "stuff." The best thing for them might be to give them a gentle kick in the butt. But if you judge that it's not okay to make them feel put on the spot, or your "need" to keep everything smooth takes over, then you may not be present to yourself, to them, or to what the moment is calling for. This can be a fine line, and the other extreme can be just as bad—or worse. However, on a deep level, I think we always know. Do you sometimes see yourself in this picture?

***Need #8:* The Need to be "Right"**

Mmm. . . Personally, I don't know anything about this one. If you don't believe me, just ask my husband. J This is when someone is more focused on being "right" in a conversation than really hearing and feeling what the other person is saying. We know we are stuck in this "need" when our joy decreases. This is different from having an enlivening and inspiring debate that feels fun. Do you ever see yourself in this picture?

***Need #9:* The Need to Feel Happy All the Time**

Often, women feel like they always have to have a cheery smile on when interacting with someone else. They feel the moment always has to be light and that if it's not, it's their job to lighten the mood. This also traps you in your own judgment of the moment and takes you out of being totally present with the other person. Do you ever see yourself in this picture?

***Need #10*: The Need to Detach from your Own Emotions and Other People's Emotions.**

Some people think that detaching from feeling emotions is the "spiritual way." People want you to "feel" them, no matter what they are emoting in the moment. People want to feel how you are feeling, too. The personality types that are often prone to getting stuck in this "need" are good at "holding space" for other people and are good observers, but they may find that they don't have a lot of close friends because they have a hard time showing their vulnerability, and really opening up to others. Do you ever see yourself in this picture?

The easiest way to discern the difference between a "need" that takes you out of being present and an impulse to share something that is being inspired by your presence is to feel your "Joy Meter." If your joy in the conversation starts to drop, or if you get bored or frustrated, you know you are in one of your "needs." If your energy rises and it's easy to feel a lot of love for the person you are talking to, without anything needing to be different, then you are in the moment.

EXERCISE #35

Which of the 10 most common "needs" do you notice are the ones you fall into the most?

What other "needs" sometimes arise in your conversations that keep you from being present?

As you move out in the world with your business, your projects, and your community and social events, remember that most of your magnetic presence comes from how present you are in any given moment. Presence—or the lack thereof—is both your greatest obstacle to truly embodying a powerful *and* feminine state and the greatest gift you can offer the world around you. There is a lot to *do* in the world, but it's your presence—the ability to *be*— that has the power to heal anything.

CHAPTER EIGHTEEN SUMMARY

Your ability to live in harmony with the rest of the planet— *and* to affect it with your positive mark of feminine power— all boils down to how present you are. There are three main areas you need to be present with in order to be the powerful *and* feminine woman you want to be:

1. Be present with your mission in the world.
2. Be present with your decisions.
3. Be present in conversation and conflict.